THE HUMANIZERS

Breathing Life
Into
AI-Generated
Content

ANDY O'BRYAN

DISCLAIMER

FOREWORD

By Declan Dunn

I'm afraid to write this foreword because the addictive allure of AI is moving so many to stop writing, and just let AI do the work.

I'm also afraid because I must write words that sum up The Humanizers, which means I must dive inside.

Even though I create The AI Optimist podcast, written 15 books, a play, endless marketing copy, and consider myself a writer from birth, I need help.

AI doesn't come close to what you'll find inside, it gives you someone else's answers. Easy yes, but you miss the personal discovery of writing.

The Humanizers teaches me to do this in a focused guide helping me connect to you, the readers and writers to be.

Reading all the hype about AI, you would think that humans are doomed to be replaced by machines.

It feels like the old Star Trek story of the Borg, where everyone looks and sounds the same - "Resistance is futile."

Or it might be a Darwinian Leap into a better future for all of us, by allowing us the time and space to write, discover, and share what Oscar Wilde put so well:

"Be yourself; everyone else is already taken."

The Humanizers moves you from the AI myth to the reason it's important for people to keep writing.

What if we didn't have the work of Oscar Wilde, but simply vanilla AI Wilde, taking a shortcut because it's easier than exploring creativity?

The Humanizers tackles this question head on for you, to preserve what your words will bring to us all.

This book takes you by the hand, using AI for idea generating and editing. The simple approach to using AI the right way, to help you as a virtual editor, brainstorming partner, and tool.

Write first and then uses ChatGPT to summarize, expand, or critique your work.

- Use AI to show blind spots and logical gaps to improve vocabulary/phrasing and find new angles.
- Let AI challenge your ideas and improve your writing, not writing for you, but with you.
- Get help from AI for analogies, creative words, and testing ideas.
- The key is using AI as a "co-pilot" to augment your skills, not replace them.

The Humanizers gives you the blueprint to do this with the SOUL Framework (Sensitivity, Openness, Understanding, and Leadership).

Chapter 4 will help you blow away the competition by discovering who you are and what you bring: "The answer lies in humanizing your approach—bringing emotion, empathy, and understanding to every piece of content you create."

How do we do that? By doing the writing, the uncomfortable time when you don't know what to write.

It's that doubt, that humility, which brings out your hidden voice.

Want to know how to stand out in the AI Age, where so much of what we read is generated automatically based on what others have written?

Dive into yourself, your experience, and share what you find.

This book is like scuba diving your creative soul, with sage advice that brings out those words inside you.

It acts like your scuba writing instructor, not pushing you into too deep, and showing you the way with everything laid out in a practical map.

Because if you let AI do the work for you, your ability to communicate and touch people with your words fades away.

Today no one uses maps, AI shows us the way – and that's a good thing. But AI can't show you how to write because it's a process, not specific directions on a map.

I used the SOUL framework to craft this forward, guiding me better than AI because this book practices what it preaches.

The Humanizers isn't just a strategy to write better. It's a call to action, to you.

We need your voice, and your writing needs to connect to people with your unique, vibrant experience.

Join the Humanizers movement and add your unique words to our culture, to our lives, and take a risk to be yourself.

Take a chance to learn to write in the voice that only you can bring. While AI is powerful as a tool and assistant, it's not alive. You are, and that's what I love about this book. It brings your words to life in a way that will change you from the moment you start following the steps.

The Humanizers is a movement to preserve and amplify our voices, our experiences, and our legacies.

The aim is preserving human creativity, empathy, and connection!

Take the chance, the time, and the patience to discover the unique, original recipe that is your life.

Time to share your words now; AI is a wakeup call to the wonder of the human imagination.

Be yourself!

TABLE OF CONTENTS

THE HUMAN SPARK IN AN AGE OF AI

W hat a time to be alive. AI has transformed how we write, create, and communicate. Large language models have ushered in unprecedented levels of efficiency, speed, and an almost magical ability to generate copy at the click of a button.

It's a powerful tool, no doubt. But as we dive headfirst into this AI-driven world, there's a looming question we can't afford to ignore: what happens when we let AI do all the work?

There's a seductive appeal to handing over the reins to automation. After all, why spend hours crafting the perfect email, blog post, or sales letter when AI can churn out something good enough in seconds? It's easy, convenient, and in a fast-moving world, it feels like a legitimate shortcut to success. But shortcuts often come at a cost, and in this case, the cost is far greater than we realize.

We are on a slippery slope.

When we rely on AI to do the heavy lifting of creativity, we risk losing a huge part of ourselves—our muse, our creative spark, that elusive thread of humanity that can't be replicated by code. It's a dangerous game, and the stakes are high: our very ability to connect authentically with those around us.

Every time we choose convenience over creativity, we move one step closer to letting go of what makes us truly human.

The Ethical Imperative of Humanizing AI Outputs

Make no mistake, this isn't just about artistic expression or personal satisfaction. This is an ethical issue. When we allow AI to generate content that lacks heart, we're not just risking our brand's integrity—we're diluting the quality of communication in society itself.

Human connection is not a luxury; it's the very fabric of meaningful interaction. If we let AI dominate without interweaving our own experiences, emotions, and empathy, we're guilty of contributing to a culture of shallow, disconnected interactions.

We cannot afford to lose sight of the fact that our audience deserves more than artificially-generated words. They deserve content that resonates, that stirs something deeper in themselves. Allowing AI to dominate without human intervention is both a creative and moral failing.

Are We Losing Our Creative Energy?

Creativity was never supposed to be easy. That's why it's so valuable. In the old days, before AI, we paid our dues. We wrestled with words, fumbled with ideas, and painstakingly polished drafts until they sparkled. It wasn't efficient, but it was real. And the result was something that felt truly alive because it carried the weight of human thought and emotion.

Today, AI offers us an escape from that effort. Look at all the hours we're saving! But here's the danger: when we hand over the creative process to machines, we risk extinguishing the fire of inspiration that has fueled human progress for centuries.

It is indeed a slippery slope. One day, you're using AI to save time. The next, you're letting it think for you. And before you know it, the act of creation—the very thing that makes you a writer, a storyteller, a creator—is a distant memory.

We must fight against this erosion. We must reclaim the art of creation, not as a chore but as a vital, life-affirming practice. Because without it, we lose our souls.

Humanizing AI: A Defiant Stand

So, what's the answer? It's not about rejecting AI outright—that would be foolish. AI is an extraordinary tool capable of enhancing our work in ways we've only just begun to explore. But we must remember that AI serves us—not the other way around.

To humanize AI-generated content is to take a defiant stand. It's saying, "I refuse to let the machine take over. I refuse to let my creativity be reduced to an algorithm." By humanizing AI outputs, we infuse them with the nuance, empathy, and soul that only we can provide. We ensure that technology remains a servant—never the master.

The Fire We Must Protect

As you begin your journey through this book, remember AI is a tool to *amplify* your voice, not to replace it. The human spark, that creative fire, is fragile. And if we're not careful, it will dim. But if we nurture it, if we protect it, it will continue to light the way forward—not just for our businesses, but for the future of human connection.

This book is a clarion call. We are The Humanizers. It's time to reclaim what's ours, to bring life back into the words we create, and to ensure that the stories we tell are not just efficient—they are alive.

Who Are The Humanizers?

The Humanizers are the ones who refuse to let the soul of their work be extinguished by automation. We are entrepreneurs, creatives, marketers, and leaders who know that AI can help, but it cannot replace the human heart.

We are the pioneers of the SOUL framework—Sensitivity, Openness, Understanding, and Leadership—which has the power to guide us in every decision, ensuring that their content, their copy, and their connections are rooted in authenticity.

The Humanizers are defiant. We reject the idea that efficiency is the ultimate goal. We know that true success lies in creating content that moves people, businesses that build trust, and brands that stand for something real. And we understand that the greatest asset any business has is not its technology—but its humanity.

This is the movement. This is the future. Welcome to The Humanizers.

Chapter One

LAYING THE GROUNDWORK

Humanized copy isn't just about **sounding** human—it's about **feeling** human. It's about knowing when to shift from facts to emotions, from solutions to stories, and back again. AI might be able to replicate the tone and style, but it can't evolve with the conversation. It doesn't experience the world like we do—it doesn't feel joy, frustration, hope, fear, or any of the other multitudes of emotions. You do. That's your superpower.

AI is a fantastic tool, but it needs a human to bring out its full potential. That's why humanization is much more than just polishing or tweaking AI-generated content. It's about infusing it with **real emotional intelligence**—something no AI tool will ever be able to achieve fully. And that's why your customers will respond to you as opposed to an algorithm.

Of course, there are many AI tools out there that can *mimic* human-sounding language. They've gotten good at simulating empathy, conversational tones, and even certain emotional triggers, and every day, these tools are getting better and better.

But here's the problem: those tools can only work with what they've been fed. They analyze patterns, they replicate the tone, but they don't understand the emotions they're writing about. It's like a parrot repeating words without understanding their meaning.

AI humanization tools might get the phrasing right, but they can't interpret context the way a human can. They don't understand **nuance**, and they can't adjust in real-time based on subtle emotional cues.

For example, AI can't detect when the emotion behind a sentence should shift from hopeful to concerned based on your customer's reaction. They generate content based on data, not lived experience.

What so many people don't realize is that AI-generated content—while efficient—lacks the very thing that makes us connect as humans: emotion. And when you're trying to sell something or even just communicate, emotion is everything.

AI can spit out perfect sentences, grammatically flawless emails, and data-driven ads. But it can't **feel**. It can't understand the human experience. Your customers aren't robots—they're people with emotions, struggles, and desires. They don't just buy products—they buy solutions to their problems. They want to feel like someone understands them.

People aren't just making rational decisions when they're buying something or choosing to engage with content. Their decisions are driven by **emotion**—fear, desire, frustration, hope. AI can process logic, but it can't tap into those emotions the way we can.

People don't care about efficiency for the sake of efficiency. They care about what it means for their lives. Maybe it means getting home earlier to see their family, or being less stressed at work, or finally leaving their 9-5 and pursuing their dream of owning their own business. That's the emotional connection. That's why humanizing your copy is so important— it speaks to the **real-life impact** your product or service can have.

When your audience feels like you genuinely **understand their struggles**—that you're speaking to their personal experience—they're much more likely to trust you. And trust is the foundation of all great marketing.

AI is a tool. It helps with speed, data, and consistency. But if you rely on it too much, your content becomes soulless, like a robot reading a script. People can feel that, even subconsciously. They'll engage less, trust less, and eventually, they'll walk away.

AI can't replicate the **nuances of human experience**—the tone, the empathy, the way we can read between the lines. When you humanize your content, you rise above the faceless companies and short-sighted entrepreneurs trying to make a sale. You're someone who understands the challenges your audience faces and has a solution tailored to them.

Can Customers Really Tell the Difference?

Another important question is: "**Can customers really distinguish between AI-generated and humanized copy?**" After all, if the customer can't tell, why does it matter?

The short answer is: Yes, they can tell the difference.

Here's why:

- **Emotional Connection**: Customers may not always consciously notice if something is AI-generated, but they often *feel* the difference. Humanized content creates an emotional connection that resonates on a deeper level. When a message feels flat or robotic, it's less likely to stick.

- **Intangible Authenticity**: Authenticity is a buzzword right now—it's something people **sense** in a message. They know when someone truly understands their needs, fears, or hopes. AI can replicate the *appearance* of authenticity, but it doesn't possess the real-world empathy to create that genuine, intangible connection.

People might not consciously think, "Hey, this was written by AI," but they can definitely sense when something is off. It's subtle, but it's real. And quite often, this can mean the difference between a sale and a rejection.

Think about it like this: have you ever had a conversation where the other person was saying all the right things, but you just couldn't **connect** with them? It's not that they were wrong, but something was missing. That's what happens with AI-generated content. It can sound human, but it doesn't feel human. And that disconnect is what makes people scroll past or click away.

Trust has always been built on more than just well-crafted words and paragraphs by good copywriters—it's built on authenticity. When people feel like they're being 'talked at' rather than engaged in a genuine conversation, they won't invest. And in today's world, where AI-generated content is flooding inboxes, feeds, and ads, standing out means being **real**.

What about you? When you read something that really hits home for you, can you feel the difference? Maybe it's a personal story in an ad or a piece of content that speaks directly to a struggle you're going through. Can you relate to it more?

That's not by accident. That's because there was a person behind it, someone who understood the deeper emotional layers and cared enough to connect with you on that level. AI can't do that.

Here's the thing: AI can write, but **it doesn't care**. It doesn't have **intent** or **emotional intuition**. People can feel that in ways they don't always articulate in surveys and focus groups—but it impacts how they engage with your content and, ultimately, your brand.

The Power of Intangible Connection

It's not just the words we write; it's the **intent behind those words** that resonate with people. It's that **intangible connection**—the part of communication that makes someone feel seen, heard, and understood on a deeper level. And that's where AI falls short. It can analyze and replicate patterns, but it can't replicate the human experience.

Your audience has developed a finely-tuned radar for anything that feels forced or insincere, and when they see an AI email or ad, they can sense the absence of the **nuances of intention** that only humans can bring.

Humans infuse **personal experience** into content—drawing on our own stories, challenges, and emotional landscapes. It's about **sharing a part of yourself**. That's the **intangible connection**—it's what makes people say, "Wow, they really get me."

This connection we're talking about—it's not always in the words themselves. It's in the **energy** behind those words. Think of it like music. You can hear a perfectly played song, but if there's no emotion behind the notes, it's forgettable. Conversely, if the musician plays with passion, even if they hit a wrong note, it resonates. That's what humanized content does—it resonates because it's *alive*.

Real connection is built on shared emotions, shared experiences, and a **human understanding** of what your audience is going through. AI can process the logic, but **we're the ones who bring the heart**.

Subconscious Pattern Recognition

Humans are incredibly adept at recognizing patterns and identifying when something doesn't quite fit, even on a subconscious level. AI-generated content often follows strict patterns based on algorithms.

While this consistency can be beneficial for efficiency, it can also make the content feel **repetitive** or **unnatural**. The human brain picks up on this lack of variation, triggering the feeling that something is artificial.

Linguistic Imperfections

Interestingly, **imperfections**—typos, minor grammar mistakes, or slightly awkward phrasing—can actually make the content feel more human. AI, by contrast, tends to generate **flawless** text.

While perfection might seem like a good thing, it can actually cause readers to **disconnect** because humans expect a certain level of natural imperfection in communication.

Contextual Awareness

Humans can process **context** in ways AI struggles to match. For example, we understand cultural references, historical context, and the unspoken feelings behind words.

AI can misinterpret or miss these cues altogether, which can lead to content that feels tone-deaf or misaligned with the audience's current emotional or social environment.

Why This Intangible Connection Matters

The future isn't about choosing between AI and humans—it's about finding a way for them to work together. AI, with its constantly new advancements, will always need **human hands and hearts** to bring its content to life. Without that human touch, everything falls flat.

This unspoken "AI radar" that customers have for discerning AI-generated content from human-generated content is rooted in several **psychological and emotional cues** that we, as humans, have been developing over millennia, and it's improving at a rapid pace with the ubiquity of AI in everything we consume.

Action Step: Reflect on your own use of technology in your business or creative processes. Ask yourself: Has automation or efficiency come at the expense of personal connection? Identify one area where you can reintegrate a human touch, whether it's a client interaction, a piece of content, or a team collaboration.

Chapter Two

THE FINANCIAL IMPACT OF HUMANIZED CONTENT

These days, content creation is often viewed through two distinct lenses: financial and ethical. On one side, companies seek efficiency, scalability, and profitability—maximizing output while minimizing costs. On the other, there's an ethical responsibility to create content that is genuine, empathetic, and human-centered, fostering trust and meaningful connections.

These two imperatives—financial gain and ethical responsibility—are often seen as opposing forces, pulling businesses in different directions. However, as we go deeper into the role of humanized content, it becomes clear that the true path to success lies in balancing both.

Humanizing AI-generated content is not just a moral or ethical choice; it's a strategic financial decision that has a direct impact on brand loyalty, customer retention, and long-term revenue.

When we talk about humanizing content, we aren't just talking about making it more relatable—we're talking about aligning business objectives with deeper human values.

At first glance, these two goals may seem incompatible. How can a business maintain profitability while also creating authentic, human-centered messaging? Is it possible to automate content creation for efficiency without losing the emotional nuances that resonate with people?

In the next two chapters, we'll explore the intersection of these two forces. We'll examine how ethical humanization can enhance financial performance and how, paradoxically, businesses that prioritize empathy and authenticity can often achieve greater financial rewards than those that solely focus on short-term profits. Striking this balance is more than just "doing the right thing"—it's about doing the *smart* thing for your business.

By understanding the dual impact of humanized content, you'll see how ethics and profitability are not mutually exclusive. Instead, when harnessed correctly, they can drive each other forward, creating not only a more connected and trustworthy brand but also a more financially resilient one.

These days, it's tempting to believe that faster content creation leads to better business outcomes. AI can generate copy in seconds, churning out articles, sales emails, and social media posts with unprecedented speed. But while AI delivers quantity, it often leaves quality—and connection—by the wayside. And it's precisely that human connection that determines whether a business thrives or falters.

Humanized content is about building trust and connection. AI can't do that. At least not in the way that humans can. Trust is the foundation of every sale, every partnership, and every loyal customer relationship.

Without trust, there is no conversion. Without connection, there is no loyalty. And without humanization, these pillars begin to crumble.

The financial impact of humanized content goes beyond mere efficiency. Sure, AI might save you time—but at what cost? If your content feels robotic, sterile, and disconnected, you'll lose the edge that separates you from the competition. You'll leave money on the table.

Studies show that emotionally connected customers are more valuable—they spend more, return more often, and recommend your brand to others. In a world of automation, it's this emotional connection that makes the difference between a one-time transaction and a long-term customer relationship.

Humanized Content Drives Conversions

AI can generate leads, but it's humanized content that turns those leads into loyal customers. When your messaging resonates emotionally, you reduce friction in the buying process. People make purchasing decisions based on how they *feel*—trust, connection, and emotion are the true drivers of sales. If your content feels artificial (like AI always will be) or detached, as if anyone could have written it, you'll lose that advantage.

Brands that embrace humanized content are seeing the results. When businesses shift from robotic, automated messaging to content that focuses on real customer stories, emotions, and deeper pain points, their conversions increase by as much as 30%. That's the power of connecting on an emotional level. But short-term sales boosts are one thing—we're talking about long-term loyalty, higher retention rates, and a reputation that builds trust over time.

Long-Term Revenue and Brand Loyalty

AI may be faster (often a lot faster), but it's a tortoise and hare scenario. In your race for efficiency, you might be sacrificing profitability. Customers aren't just looking for the cheapest option or the fastest response—they're looking for brands they can trust: brands that make them feel seen, understood, and valued. Humanized content is the key to unlocking that trust.

Creating content that resonates, that moves people to take action, and that builds lasting relationships is what will separate you from the rest of the pack. When you shift your focus from speed to connection, you'll see the real impact on your bottom line.

Humanization as the Pilot Light of Connection

Humanization is that small flame that keeps the fire of your brand alive, ready to ignite something bigger. Like the pilot light in a furnace, it's often overlooked, but without it, the entire system becomes cold and lifeless. AI may be the engine that drives your content machine, but without that spark of humanity, your messaging loses its warmth, its soul, and its ability to connect with real people.

In every piece of content, there's an opportunity to include a small but crucial element of humanization—a tone of empathy, a personal story, or a genuine attempt to connect. These might seem like small details, but they are the key to keeping the emotional fire burning in your brand relationships. Without them, you risk your content becoming just another automated message lost in the noise.

The pilot light of humanization is always burning, even when the larger system is running on autopilot. It's a constant reminder that business is personal. Behind every transaction every decision, is a human being looking to connect with something real. And as long as that flame is there, your brand will never go cold.

The Path of Least Resistance

In today's content landscape, writing has become commoditized. It's sad. AI has democratized the act of writing, and in doing so, it has stripped it of its emotional depth. What was once an art form—a craft honed over years of experience—has now become a mass-produced product, cranked out at a moment's notice by algorithms designed to prioritize speed over substance. And while AI has made writing easier, it has also led to a *crisis of quality*.

In the rush to create more content, businesses are sacrificing the very thing that makes their messaging valuable: authenticity. The result? A wave of mediocrity flooding the market, where content blends into a sea of sameness, devoid of the personality and emotional connection that once defined great writing.

The Crisis of Quality

As businesses prioritize quantity over quality, the audience suffers from content fatigue. People are scrolling past automated posts that all sound the same—void of personality, emotion, and connection. This content crisis is creating a loss of connection between brands and their audiences. AI may be able to write content, but it cannot create the relationships that drive real engagement and loyalty.

This shift has led to stagnating sales, disillusioned customers, and a growing awareness that AI-generated content is missing something vital. Humanization is no longer a luxury—it is a necessity. Businesses that fail to humanize their content risk becoming irrelevant in a world where consumers crave authentic connections.

The Pain of Authentic Writing

Authentic writing was never supposed to be easy. Crafting content that resonates with readers, touches their hearts, and inspires them to take action requires emotional labor. It requires vulnerability, empathy, and an understanding of human nature that no machine can replicate. The struggle to find the right words to connect deeply with your audience is what gives writing its meaning. And that's what AI lacks.

AI has become a crutch. What was once a tool to assist writers is now being used to replace them. In the rush to produce more content at a faster rate, businesses are losing sight of what really matters: the human connection that makes their work valuable in the first place.

This is the wake-up call. More content doesn't mean better results. The over-reliance on AI is leading to a collapse of quality, and audiences are tired of robotic messages. It's time to slow down, to be intentional, and to remember that the value of content lies not in its speed but in its ability to connect.

Chapter Three

THE ETHICAL IMPERATIVE OF HUMANIZING AI-GENERATED CONTENT

W e live in a time when the line between humans and machines is increasingly blurred. AI promises to automate, optimize, and scale the process of communication, but at what cost? We are not merely dealing with tools of convenience—we are facing an existential crossroads for creativity, empathy, and the core of human connection.

The ethical imperative to humanize AI-generated content isn't just a nice-to-have; it is a moral responsibility. Failure to act in this direction risks not only dehumanizing communication but also surrendering our creative essence to algorithms. This is not a matter of convenience—it's a matter of survival for what it means to be human.

The Moral Responsibility of Sensitivity in a Mechanized World

Simply put, AI is indifferent to human nuance. Its algorithms are programmed to identify patterns, and yet, it does so with an almost clinical precision devoid of emotion, culture, or lived experience. The beauty of human sensitivity—the ability to read between the lines, to perceive the intangible essence of what makes us connect—is entirely absent in AI.

We must ask ourselves: Is it enough to create content that merely serves its functional purpose, or must we insist on preserving the art of emotional connection?

Human sensitivity, the very thing that makes us *human*, cannot be replicated by AI, no matter how sophisticated its neural networks are. To allow machines to take over the delicate fabric of our communications without safeguarding this sensitivity is to pave the way for a world where cold efficiency supersedes empathy. And in a world where empathy is lost, what remains?

The real question, then, is: Do we want to live in a world where content is stripped of its soul, where efficiency erodes emotional resonance, and where our interactions are reduced to transactions?

Or will we defy this dehumanization?

The Silent Perpetuation of Bias: A Moral Failure

Let's go deeper into one of the more insidious issues with AI-generated content: bias. It is well-documented that AI systems can unintentionally perpetuate societal biases, magnifying disparities that have plagued us for centuries. But why is this happening?

The answer is simple: AI learns from us.

It mirrors our data, our actions, and our histories. It reflects back the biases embedded in the datasets it consumes. If the content it produces fails to challenge those biases, then AI becomes not only a tool of convenience but a mechanism of oppression. It acts as an amplifier for the very problems we claim to want to solve—discrimination, exclusion, and inequality.

Let's consider a real-world example. In 2018, Amazon scrapped an AI recruiting tool because it was found to be biased against women. The system, trained on resumes submitted over the previous decade, was designed to identify the most qualified candidates. However, because the data set reflected a male-dominated workforce, the AI systematically downranked resumes that included the word "women's" and penalized graduates from all women's colleges.

Here, the ethical question looms large: *Who is responsible when AI goes wrong?*

The answer, though uncomfortable, is clear—it's us. We cannot delegate ethical responsibility to machines. The bias is not in the AI itself; it's in the data, in the training, and in the systems we create. And as creators of these systems, we have a moral duty to ensure that the content we produce through AI isn't merely effective but just, fair, and representative.

Transparency: The Hidden Crisis of Trust

We're not just talking about creating content—we're talking about trust, a word that keeps popping up here for a reason. Every piece of communication builds or breaks the trust between the creator and the consumer. The rise of AI has the potential to upend this delicate balance.

Consider this: when we engage with content, we naturally assume there's a human behind it. The words we read, the messages we receive— they feel personal because we expect them to come from another human mind. But what happens when AI enters the scene? When the content that feels human is, in fact, the work of a machine, does that trust remain intact?

This brings us to the issue of transparency. Do audiences have the right to know when they're interacting with AI-generated content? Is it ethical to create content without disclosing its artificial origins?

With AI increasingly responsible for communication, failing to disclose the source of that content is a betrayal of trust. It manipulates the reader into believing they are connecting with another human when, in reality, they are engaging with an algorithm designed for maximum engagement. The deception, while subtle, corrodes the foundation of authentic human communication.

Defending Creativity: The Last Bastion of Humanity

Creativity is humanity's final frontier. It is the force that has propelled our evolution—from cave paintings to symphonies, from the written word to digital art. It is our most profound expression of individuality, and yet it is also the aspect of our humanity most threatened by AI.

Let's be clear: AI cannot create in the way we do. It can mimic, replicate, and simulate, but it cannot *originate*. Every creative output it produces is the result of an algorithmic pattern—an all-you-can-eat buffet of existing data devoid of true innovation. This is a critical distinction.

To cede our creative powers to AI is to abdicate our most sacred responsibility: the act of creation itself.

Yes, AI can assist in the creative process. It can help us ideate faster, draft quicker, and produce at a scale previously unimaginable. But it is our ethical duty to ensure that AI serves as a tool, not as a replacement for human creativity. Automation can make the mundane aspects of creation easier, but it should never replace the spontaneous, intuitive, and deeply personal nature of human innovation.

If we allow AI to take over the creative process, we lose the very thing that sets us apart from the machines: our capacity to create meaning from nothing, to breathe life into our ideas, and to inspire and move others.

We cannot—*we must not*—allow AI to commoditize creativity. To do so would be to betray the very essence of what it means to be human.

The Empathy Deficit: A Call to Arms

At the heart of human communication lies empathy. It is what allows us to transcend mere transactions and connect on a deeper emotional level. It is the ability to understand, to share, and to care. AI cannot feel; it cannot empathize.

And yet, we find ourselves in a world where AI is increasingly being used to generate messages that are intended to be empathetic. How can a machine that doesn't feel attempt to replicate the nuances of human emotion?

This goes way beyond a technical limitation; it is an ethical crisis. We are at risk of losing our emotional literacy if we allow machines to handle the bulk of our communication. When we automate empathy, we lose our ability to practice it ourselves. The very act of communicating—of listening, responding, and understanding—becomes mechanized, and with that, we risk losing our capacity for genuine human connection.

The ethical imperative is clear: Empathy must remain a human endeavor. We must not outsource our emotional intelligence to machines. To do so is to abandon one of the most fundamental aspects of our humanity.

Defying the Automation of Humanity

The future of content creation is not just about efficiency or scalability—it's about survival, not of the machines, but of us. If we continue down a path where AI-generated content is accepted as the norm without human oversight, without ethical considerations, and without a commitment to humanization, we risk losing the very essence of what makes us human.

And even though this book is primarily for marketers, writers, authors and other creative entrepreneurs, the overarching message is a call to arms for all of humanity.

The rise of AI forces us to confront the fundamental question: *What kind of world do we want to live in?* A world where machines control the narrative, where creativity is commodified, and where empathy is algorithmically generated? Or a world where AI serves as a tool—a powerful, efficient tool—but one that is always guided by human hands and hearts?

We have the power to choose. And that choice, at its core, is an ethical one.

Action Step: Consider the AI tools or systems you use in your business. Are there any that you rely on too heavily? Create a list of human-centered practices you can implement to balance technology and personal interaction, ensuring your work remains empathetic and relational.

Chapter Four

THE HUMANIZERS' SOUL FRAMEWORK

Now that we've laid down the gauntlet, you might be wondering: **how can I differentiate myself** when machines create the majority of copy and content? The answer lies in **humanizing** your approach—bringing emotion, empathy, and understanding to every piece of content you create.

At the core of this book, and the **Humanizers movement**, is the SOUL Framework. This is the blueprint for how you can consistently **bring humanity** into AI-generated copy. The framework is a set of techniques, but it's also a philosophy that will help you tap into the **deep, emotional connection** that every successful piece of content needs to make.

What is the SOUL Framework

SOUL stands for **Sensitivity, Openness, Understanding,** and **Leadership**—four pillars that serve as the foundation of all humanized content.

Let's break each of these down and explore how they apply to creating copy and content that resonates on a human level.

1. Sensitivity: Listening to the Audience's Emotions

Sensitivity has multiple meanings, but in the marketing world, it means a lot more than just being aware of what your audience wants—it's about tapping into their **emotional state**. Sensitivity in content creation means paying attention to the subtle cues in your audience's behavior and responding with messages that resonate deeply.

For example, instead of simply writing copy that highlights the features of a product, a sensitive writer digs deeper into the emotional reasons why someone might want that product.

What are their frustrations?

What are their struggles?

What are their aspirations?

AI can suggest features and benefits, but it takes a human to understand how those benefits solve deeply felt problems.

Consider a company that sells time-management software. AI might write a generic ad listing the software's features, but a Humanizer would frame it like this:

"Imagine no longer waking up in the middle of the night, stressing about all the tasks you didn't get to. With our software, you can organize your day in a way that frees up time for the things that matter most to you—your family, your passions, your life."

This approach speaks to the **emotional desires** of the audience, not just their rational need for a productivity tool.

Of course, with the right prompt, AI can do that too, but in the time it takes you to craft that prompt or have AI perform multiple revisions, you could have humanized it for better results.

2. Openness: Welcoming Feedback and Adaptation

Openness is the second pillar of the SOUL Framework. It's about remaining flexible and welcoming feedback—whether it's from your audience, team members, or even the data you collect.

In humanized content creation, **openness** means being willing to adapt based on the **emotional feedback** you're getting from your audience. It's about asking questions like:

What are my audience's real pain points?

What would it feel like to walk a mile in their shoes?

How can I adjust my messaging to better connect with them emotionally?

AI is great at data collection and interpreting our prompts, but it's **human insight** that helps us translate that data into meaningful action.

When you remain open to feedback, you can constantly **refine your message** to make it more human and more relevant to the people you're trying to reach.

Say your blog content is getting lots of views but few comments or shares. An open-minded Humanizer would review the feedback and ask:

Am I striking the right emotional tone?

Am I connecting with my audience's deeper needs, or am I staying too surface-level?

This openness leads to better, more **resonant content** over time.

3. Understanding: Knowing Your Audience Beyond the Surface

Understanding goes beyond demographics—it's about truly **knowing** your audience's dreams, fears, and motivations. It requires the ability to put yourself in their position and write from a place of deep empathy.

AI can gather all kinds of data about your target audience, but it can't grasp the **emotional nuance** of their lived experiences. Understanding your audience means befriending them, becoming deeply aware of their challenges, and then speaking to those challenges in ways that only a human can.

If you're marketing a fitness program, for example, you could rely on AI to target people based on age, income, and fitness goals. But a Humanizer would go deeper:

Why is this person really seeking fitness?

Are they recovering from an injury? Trying to boost their self-esteem? Looking for a community of like-minded people?

By understanding the **emotional reasons** behind their goals, you can craft copy that hits home on a personal level, like this:

"This is so much more than getting in shape—this is really all about reclaiming your confidence, your energy, and the belief that you can achieve anything you set your mind to."

4. Leadership: Guiding with Empathy and Authority

Finally, **Leadership** is about **guiding your audience** with a sense of authority but with empathy at the forefront. Humanized content creators take on the role of a **trusted guide**—offering solutions, inspiration, and insight while showing genuine care for their audience's well-being.

AI can generate instructional content, but it takes a human to provide **empathetic leadership**. People want to feel like they're being led by someone who understands their journey, not just someone who's throwing solutions at them.

"You don't need another fitness app. What you need is a clear path guided by someone who's been there and knows first-hand how hard it is to get started. We're here to help you every step of the way—not just with workouts (anyone can offer that), but with motivation and support that's with you for the long haul."

See what I mean? Leading with **empathy** shows that you're more than just an expert—you're a **partner in their success**.

The SOUL Framework In Action

Each element of the **SOUL Framework**—Sensitivity, Openness, Understanding, and Leadership—works together to form the foundation of **humanized content creation**. By weaving these pillars into every aspect of your writing, you can create content that **feels personal** and deeply **resonates with your audience**.

This is what separates a **Humanizer** from the sea of AI-generated copy. Producing content is one thing. This is all about producing **connection**. And when your audience feels that connection, they're more likely to engage, to trust, and ultimately, to convert.

Later in this book we'll dive deeper into the SOUL Framework to show you how to apply it in your marketing efforts.

In the next chapter, we'll explore the **specific emotions** that AI cannot replicate and how you can use these emotions to create content that goes beyond the surface and touches the **hearts and minds** of your audience.

Action Step: Apply the SOUL Framework to one of your current or future marketing elements, then examine the before and after of it to see how it evolved. If you like, run an A/B test of the old, current, revised text to see if your conversion rates improved.

Chapter Five

EMOTION IN COPYWRITING – WHAT AI CAN'T IMITATE

Human emotions are what make stories resonate, and when it comes to **copywriting**, these emotions are the glue that connects you to your audience. By now, you know that AI can replicate patterns, analyze data, and even mimic human language.

But the real magic of copywriting comes from tapping into emotions that are uniquely **human**—emotions that machines can't understand or feel. In this chapter, we'll explore the key emotions that make copy come alive and how you can use them to create **impactful, humanized content**.

Why Emotions Are Essential to Copywriting

Think about some of the most memorable pieces of copy you've come across. Maybe it was an ad that tugged at your heartstrings or a tagline that made you stop in your tracks. What made it stand out? It wasn't just the information it provided—it was the **emotional response** it evoked.

Humans are emotional beings, and our decisions—whether we realize it or not—are often driven by how we feel. Logic may justify a purchase, but it's an emotion that compels us to act. AI-generated content, while efficient, often lacks this emotional spark. It can craft logical arguments and generate perfectly structured sentences, but it can't replicate the **emotional depth** that makes a piece of content truly memorable.

The Limits of AI and the Emotional Depth Only Humans Can Reach

As advanced as AI becomes, there are emotional experiences it can't fully comprehend or emulate. Humans possess an intricate emotional landscape that involves multitudes of complex feelings, contradictions, and depth.

To create copy that truly resonates, you need to tap into emotions that **AI simply can't touch**. These are the emotions that make people feel understood, valued, and connected. Let's break down 50 key emotions that every Humanizer should understand and apply in their copy.

50 Business-Related Emotions That AI Can't Replicate

1. **Nostalgia**
   AI lacks personal memories and the emotional context of the past that create deep connections to experiences, making it impossible to trigger true nostalgic feelings.

2. **Empathy**
   This involves understanding another person's unique emotional experience, which AI cannot genuinely grasp because it lacks human emotional intuition.

3. **Anticipation**

   A future-oriented emotion tied to personal expectations and excitement, which AI can neither experience nor authentically convey.

4. **Regret**

   AI doesn't have personal experiences or emotions tied to missed opportunities and, therefore, cannot fully understand or convey regret.

5. **Triumph**

   The emotional reward after overcoming challenges requires personal effort and struggle—something AI doesn't experience.

6. **Awe**

   Stems from a sense of wonder and admiration for something extraordinary, which AI can't authentically feel or convey without emotional depth.

7. **Relief**

   Felt after overcoming tension or stress, but AI doesn't have the capacity to experience personal stress or relief from it.

8. **Love**

   Deeply personal, tied to human bonds and emotional investment, which are foreign concepts to AI.

9. **Curiosity**

   Drives humans to seek new information and experiences, but AI doesn't possess the innate desire to explore beyond its programming.

10. **Contentment**

Comes from a deep sense of satisfaction, often after achieving balance or success—emotions that go beyond data or factual outcomes.

11. **Authentic Gratitude**

Requires genuine emotional appreciation, which AI cannot experience as it lacks emotional context and personal relationships.

12. **Vulnerability**

Involves the conscious decision to open oneself up to risk or emotional exposure, something AI cannot understand because it doesn't have emotional stakes.

13. **Forgiveness**

A complex human process that involves emotional healing and growth, which is beyond AI's ability to navigate.

14. **Spontaneous Joy**

Unpredictable and deeply felt, joy often emerges from personal interactions or experiences that AI cannot partake in or initiate.

15. **Moral Dilemmas**

Requires emotional and ethical discernment, which AI lacks because it operates on logic without personal moral or emotional contexts.

16. **Personal Sacrifice**

Involves emotional conflict and the decision to give something up for a greater good, which AI cannot experience or fully comprehend.

17. **Bittersweet Victory**

    The duality of emotions—joy mixed with sadness—is a uniquely human experience that AI cannot replicate due to its lack of emotional depth.

18. **Redemption**

    A journey of emotional growth and recovery, which AI cannot genuinely portray or experience since it lacks a personal moral framework.

19. **Generosity without Expectation**

    A pure act of giving that involves empathy and selflessness, emotions that AI cannot authentically experience.

20. **Euphoria from Creative Accomplishment**

    The emotional high after completing a creative project is tied to personal investment and satisfaction, which AI lacks.

21. **Complex Guilt**

    Involves emotional weight, moral judgment, and personal reflection—emotions that are beyond AI's capacity to feel or convey.

22. **True Empathy**

    Requires shared human experiences and the ability to feel someone else's emotions, which AI lacks entirely.

23. **Sorrow Mixed with Acceptance**

    A complex blend of grief and acceptance, an emotional duality that AI cannot grasp or recreate.

24. Passion-Driven Risk

The emotional drive to pursue an uncertain outcome for a personal vision or goal, which AI cannot replicate or appreciate.

25. Compassion Fatigue

Emotional exhaustion from giving too much of oneself—something AI can simulate but cannot experience.

26. Bitterness and Resentment

The long-term emotional impact of being wronged requires personal emotional experience to comprehend fully.

27. Transcendent Love

The unconditional, all-encompassing love for something greater than oneself, a deeply human emotional state.

28. Pride in Overcoming Adversity

Involves the emotional journey of persevering through challenges, which AI can't experience since it has no personal investment or struggle.

29. Inner Conflict

The emotional tension of being torn between two desires requires human emotional depth and introspection.

30. Professional Pride

Comes from personal effort, skill, and achievement in one's work—an emotional state that AI can't experience.

31. Ownership and Responsibility

Involves the emotional weight and personal investment of being accountable for decisions and outcomes beyond AI's understanding.

32. **Entrepreneurial Passion**

    Driven by a deep emotional connection to one's vision, which AI cannot share or understand.

33. **Resilience in the Face of Setbacks**

    Requires emotional endurance and persistence, qualities that AI does not possess.

34. **Fear of Business Failure**

    The anxiety and emotional burden of facing financial uncertainty, which AI cannot experience or alleviate emotionally.

35. **Relief After Crisis Management**

    Comes from the emotional release after navigating a difficult situation, a feeling AI cannot authentically understand.

36. **Client Connection and Trust**

    Built through emotional bonds and personal relationships, which AI can assist with but cannot fully create or experience.

37. **Competitive Drive**

    Fueled by personal ambition and emotional grit, qualities that AI cannot replicate or be motivated by.

38. **Fulfillment from Mentorship**

    The emotional reward from helping others succeed is something AI cannot experience or authentically convey.

39. **Passion for Innovation**

    Driven by excitement, vision, and emotional investment in creating something new, which AI cannot feel or express.

40. **Empathy for Employees**

Requires understanding the emotional needs of others in a workplace, something AI cannot feel or navigate with human nuance.

41. **Courage to Take Risks**

Emotional bravery to pursue uncertain outcomes is something AI can't experience since it lacks personal stakes.

42. **Frustration with Bureaucracy**

The emotional irritation of navigating complex systems, which requires personal experience and emotional patience, AI cannot replicate.

43. **Collaboration Excitement**

The shared emotional energy in a collaborative team effort, which AI can assist with but not fully experience.

44. **Relief After a Major Deadline**

The deep emotional release after completing a major task is a feeling that AI cannot experience or fully simulate.

45. **Loyalty to a Brand or Business**

Built through emotional commitment and personal experiences, qualities that AI cannot authentically feel.

46. **Emotional Investment in a Product**

The pride and emotional connection tied to creating something that AI can't experience.

47. **Perseverance in the Face of Uncertainty**

The emotional determination to keep going despite uncertain outcomes is something AI cannot feel.

48. **Sense of Achievement After a Long Journey**

The profound pride and emotional satisfaction that comes from completing a long-term goal, which AI cannot experience.

49. **Gratification from Customer Success**

The emotional reward from seeing others succeed with your help, which AI cannot replicate or feel.

50. **Tenacity in Overcoming Rejection**

The emotional resilience to keep going despite failure which requires a depth of feeling and personal investment that AI doesn't have.

Using Human Emotions to Your Advantage

As a Humanizer, your job is to tap into these and many other **human-only emotions** and bring them into your content in a way that resonates with your audience. Emotions are powerful motivators, and when you write with these in mind, you create content that not only informs but also **connects**.

By weaving these emotions into your copy, you're **creating an experience** for your audience. And that's what makes humanized content stand out in a world flooded with AI-generated noise.

Moving Forward

Now that we've explored the key emotions that AI can't replicate, the next step is to learn how to identify **robotic content** and transform it into something human. In the next chapter, we'll dive into practical techniques for spotting AI-generated copy and turning it into emotionally resonant, humanized content.

Action Step:

Choose one aspect of your business or creative process where you can focus on humanization. Make a specific plan for how you will integrate more intentional, human-driven interactions in that area. This could be with clients, customers, or your own team.

Chapter Six

HOW TO IDENTIFY AND HUMANIZE AI-GENERATED COPY

With AI being used across nearly every industry, content generation has become easier, faster, and more scalable than ever before. But as you've probably noticed, there's a downside: much of this content feels **generic, impersonal, and robotic.**

In this chapter, we'll walk through how to identify **AI-generated content** that lacks a human touch, and I'll show you how to transform that content into something that speaks directly to your audience's **emotions and needs**. It's time to bridge the gap between **automation** and **authenticity**.

Why AI-Generated Copy Falls Flat

To understand how to improve AI-generated content, we first need to understand where it falls short. AI is incredibly good at processing data and mimicking human language patterns, but it's fundamentally missing a key ingredient—**emotional intelligence**. AI doesn't have the ability to feel, empathize, or understand the complexity of human relationships and communication.

Here are some common traits of AI-generated content:

- **Lack of nuance**: AI-generated copy often sounds generic because it tries to appeal to everyone without truly understanding the audience's specific emotions or needs.

- **Stiff or awkward phrasing**: Even with natural language processing, AI still struggles to create fluid, conversational content. There's a distinct lack of **human rhythm and flow** in its language.

- **Over-reliance on data**: AI can provide facts, figures, and technical explanations, but it can't translate these into a compelling story or emotional connection.

- **Emotional flatness**: AI-generated content might address surface-level concerns but rarely explores the emotional core of the message.

Once you understand these gaps, it becomes easier to spot AI-driven content—and to know where to begin when humanizing it.

Spotting AI-Generated Content: Red Flags to Watch For

There are several key indicators that you're dealing with content written by AI. While these red flags might not be obvious at first glance, once you train yourself to notice them, you'll start to see patterns that reveal the tell-tale signs.

1. Generic Tone and Phrasing

AI-generated content often uses broad, generic phrasing that doesn't connect with a specific audience. If you see sentences that sound like they could apply to anyone, anywhere, it's a clue that the content lacks human insight.

Example:

- AI copy: *"Our software helps businesses improve productivity and efficiency."*
- Humanized version: *"Our software helps your business run smoothly, so you can focus on what matters—growing your vision without the daily grind."*

2. Awkward Transitions

AI has a hard time creating natural transitions between ideas. Sentences may feel disjointed, and there's often a lack of flow that connects one thought to the next.

Example:

- AI copy: *"We offer powerful tools. They will help you increase sales. Our software is used by businesses worldwide."*

- Humanized version: *"With our powerful tools, you'll increase sales faster than you imagined. Join thousands of businesses worldwide who are already benefiting from our streamlined software."*

3. Repetitive Structure

AI tends to reuse the same sentence structures and phrases, making the content feel robotic and monotonous. Humans naturally vary their sentence lengths and style to keep the reader engaged.

Example:

- AI copy: *"This service is fast. This service is reliable. This service is affordable."*
- Humanized version: *"Speed, reliability, and affordability—that's what makes our service stand out. When you need quick solutions without sacrificing quality, we're the partner you can trust."*

4. Lack of Emotional Appeal

As mentioned earlier, AI doesn't understand human emotions. It can generate factual information, but it struggles to connect on an emotional level.

Example:

- AI copy: *"Our software has great features and will improve your business."*
- Humanized version: *"Our software was designed to ease your workload so you can focus on what really matters—your clients, your team, and your vision for the future."*

Here are 50 overused, ubiquitous AI-generated words and phrases often found in copywriting and content creation. If you can spot them in today's marketing landscape, you can bet your customers can too:

1. Game-changer
2. Revolutionary
3. Cutting-edge
4. Next-level
5. Innovative solution

6. State-of-the-art

7. Unleash your potential

8. Transform your business

9. Maximize efficiency

10. Leverage the power of AI

11. Unlock growth

12. Streamline your workflow

13. Effortless

14. Seamless integration

15. All-in-one platform

16. Optimize your strategy

17. Results-driven

18. Take your [X] to new heights

19. Fast, easy, and reliable

20. Proven track record

21. Best-in-class

22. Unlock the full potential

23. Data-driven insights

24. Tailored for your needs

25. Scalable solutions

26. Achieve your goals

27. Boost productivity

28. Exceed expectations

29. Experience the difference

30. Future-proof your business

31. Unmatched performance

32. Comprehensive approach

33. Empower your team

34. Unparalleled results

35. Take control of your [X]

36. Turnkey solution

37. Proven to work

38. Stay ahead of the curve

39. I hope this email finds you well

40. Seamless experience

41. Customized to your needs

42. Real-time results

43. Disrupt the market

44. End-to-end solution

45. Transform the way you [X]

46. Best-kept secret

47. Power up your [X]

48. The future of [X]

49. Tailor-made for success

50. Unlock new opportunities

How to Humanize AI-Generated Content: Practical Techniques

Now that you know how to spot AI content, let's talk about how to transform it into something more human. The goal isn't to rewrite everything from scratch but rather to **inject empathy, emotion, and relatability** into existing copy.

Here's how you can do it:

1. Infuse Personality

One of the quickest ways to humanize content is by adding a **personal voice**. AI-generated content tends to err on the side of formal and dry, but by using conversational language, you can immediately make the content feel more human.

Actionable Example:

- AI copy: *"Our software has many benefits for users."*
- Humanized version: *"With our software, you'll get tools that actually make your day easier—from automating tasks to keeping everything organized."*

Tip: Think about how you would say something to a friend or colleague and apply that tone to your copy.

2. Add Empathy

Empathy is at the heart of human connection. By acknowledging your audience's feelings, frustrations, or desires, you create content that speaks directly to them.

Actionable Example:

- AI copy: *"Our service is highly efficient."*
- Humanized version: *"We know how stressful it can be to juggle a hundred tasks at once. That's why we created a service that's not just efficient but designed to make your workload lighter."*

Tip: Consider the emotions your audience might be feeling and address those feelings directly.

3. Use Storytelling Techniques

Stories are what connect us as humans. AI can provide the facts, but it's up to us to **weave those facts into a narrative** that resonates. Even a short anecdote can add layers of relatability to your content.

Actionable Example:

- AI copy: *"Our product increases productivity."*
- Humanized version: *"When Sarah, a small business owner, started using our product, she went from feeling overwhelmed by her to-do list to managing her day with ease—and now, she has more time for what really matters."*

Tip: Incorporate short stories or case studies that highlight real-world applications and outcomes. We'll be discussing storytelling more in-depth shortly.

4. Tap into Emotion

We've talked a lot about emotions because they're the core of humanized content. Make sure that your copy speaks to **human desires** like connection, security, or belonging. AI might list the features of a product, but you can show the **emotional benefits**.

Actionable Example:

- AI copy: *"Our tool is designed to improve efficiency and productivity."*
- Humanized version: *"Imagine leaving the office each day knowing you've accomplished everything you set out to do. That's the kind of peace of mind our tool provides."*

Tip: Think about the emotional outcomes your audience is seeking and build your message around those.

By learning how to spot AI-generated content and applying humanization techniques, you're not only improving the copy—you're transforming it into something that **resonates deeply** with your audience.

Humanized content stands out in a sea of automated noise because it connects emotionally, tells a story, and speaks to the reader in a way that AI simply can't.

This is where you, as a **Humanizer**, have the advantage. You can take what AI provides and elevate it into content that engages, inspires, and converts.

The future of content creation is a *partnership* between **human insight** and **AI efficiency**. Your job as a Humanizer is to take what AI can produce and enhance it with your unique ability to understand, empathize, and connect. This is the heart of humanized content creation—and this is how you'll stand out.

AI Emotional Trigger Words and Humanized Alternatives

As AI becomes more integrated into content creation, it's clear that while AI can be incredibly efficient at generating emotionally charged words, the result can often feel inauthentic or overly mechanical.

While AI-generated content may technically hit the right emotional triggers, it often lacks the nuance and subtlety that only human touch can provide. To truly connect with audiences on a deeper level, we need to balance AI efficiency with human warmth and understanding.

Below are 25 common emotional trigger words that AI may default to using, along with three alternative words or phrases that humans might naturally use instead. These humanized alternatives aim to evoke the same emotion but in a way that feels more genuine and personal, allowing for a stronger emotional connection with the reader.

1. AI Emotional Trigger Word: Excited
Human Alternative Words: Thrilled, Enthusiastic, Ecstatic

2. AI Emotional Trigger Word: Happy
Human Alternative Words: Joyful, Delighted, Content

3. AI Emotional Trigger Word: Satisfied
Human Alternative Words: Fulfilled, Contented, Pleased

4. AI Emotional Trigger Word: Anxious
Human Alternative Words: Worried, Nervous, Apprehensive

5. AI Emotional Trigger Word: Hopeful
Human Alternative Words: Optimistic, Encouraged, Expectant

6. AI Emotional Trigger Word: Curious
Human Alternative Words: Inquisitive, Interested, Intrigued

7. AI Emotional Trigger Word: Focused
Human Alternative Words: Concentrated, Attentive, Engaged

8. AI Emotional Trigger Word: Confident
Human Alternative Words: Assured, Self-assured, Positive

9. AI Emotional Trigger Word: Relaxed
Human Alternative Words: Calm, Unwound, Serene

10. AI Emotional Trigger Word: Motivated
Human Alternative Words: Driven, Inspired, Determined

11. AI Emotional Trigger Word: Impatient

Human Alternative Words: Restless, Eager, Antsy

12. AI Emotional Trigger Word: Fearful

Human Alternative Words: Scared, Terrified, Afraid

13. AI Emotional Trigger Word: Amused

Human Alternative Words: Entertained, Tickled, Charmed

14. AI Emotional Trigger Word: Disappointed

Human Alternative Words: Let down, Unhappy, Unsatisfied

15. AI Emotional Trigger Word: Optimistic

Human Alternative Words: Hopeful, Positive, Confident

16. AI Emotional Trigger Word: Insecure

Human Alternative Words: Doubtful, Unsure, Self-conscious

17. AI Emotional Trigger Word: Overwhelmed

Human Alternative Words: Swamped, Flooded, Drowned

18. AI Emotional Trigger Word: Determined

Human Alternative Words: Resolute, Committed, Steadfast

19. AI Emotional Trigger Word: Empathetic

Human Alternative Words: Understanding, Compassionate, Sympathetic

20. AI Emotional Trigger Word: Nostalgic

Human Alternative Words: Sentimental, Wistful, Fond

21. AI Emotional Trigger Word: Impressed

Human Alternative Words: Astonished, Amazed, Awed

22. AI Emotional Trigger Word: Grateful

Human Alternative Words: Thankful, Appreciative, Indebted

23. AI Emotional Trigger Word: Disheartened

Human Alternative Words: Dejected, Despondent, Discouraged

24. AI Emotional Trigger Word: Indifferent

Human Alternative Words: Apathetic, Uninterested, Lukewarm

25. AI Emotional Trigger Word: Overjoyed

Human Alternative Words: Thrilled, Elated, Over the moon

These alternative words provide a more nuanced and human touch to emotional triggers, allowing for a deeper and more relatable connection with the audience.

Chapter Seven

THE POWER OF INTUITION IN HUMANIZATION

With all this AI content out there now, one of the most overlooked yet crucial elements of humanization is **intuition**. It's more than just a "gut feeling"—intuition is a deeply ingrained sense honed through life experiences, emotional intelligence, and a connection to something larger than oneself. It's what guides our decisions when logic, data, and algorithms fail to provide the full picture.

When we talk about humanizing AI-generated content, we are talking about **preserving that sixth sense**, the instinct that tells us when something is missing or when something just *feels* right. AI can mimic human language, but it cannot replicate the **emotional compass** we rely on to navigate complex social interactions, especially in areas like copywriting, marketing, and storytelling.

Intuition is:

- **The gut instinct** that tells us when a message isn't landing, even when all the data suggests it should.
- **The sixth sense** allows us to feel the undercurrent of emotion in our audience, even if they're not expressing it overtly.
- **The creative spark** that inspires us to go off-script, to abandon the formula, and to take a risk that AI would never suggest.

Gut Instinct and Emotional Resonance

At its core, human intuition is about **emotional resonance**—the ability to sense how someone will react to what you're saying, even before you say it. This instinct allows us to **pivot** in real-time, adjusting our message, tone, or approach based on the unspoken feedback we perceive.

For example, a copywriter might look at an AI-generated promotional email and feel that, while the structure and logic are sound, the message is too cold or impersonal. They trust their gut to adjust the wording, soften the tone, or add a layer of empathy that data couldn't anticipate. The result? A message that not only informs but **moves** the reader, inspiring trust and connection.

AI can replicate structure, but only humans can craft true meaning. This ability to perceive and respond to the emotional needs of an audience is something that algorithms will never understand. It's **intangible** but **powerful**, and it's what makes humanized content stand out in a sea of automated noise.

The Sixth Sense in Storytelling and Copywriting

The concept of a **sixth sense**—that almost mystical ability to know something without being told—is vital when crafting stories or writing copy. Great storytellers don't just follow a formula; they instinctively know when to build tension, when to pull back, and when to strike an emotional chord. This sense is what transforms a good story into a **memorable one**.

In copywriting, the sixth sense allows us to feel the pulse of our audience. We know when something might be too forceful or too passive, too complex or too simplistic. This is something AI simply cannot replicate. AI may be able to suggest keywords or optimize for SEO, but it cannot sense **when a reader needs to be reassured** or **when they need to be challenged.**

Think about the way a **pilot** flies a plane. Sure, some instruments guide the flight, but seasoned pilots often rely on their **instincts** to make critical adjustments—especially in unpredictable conditions. The same is true for copywriters and content creators. Data is useful, but when you're trying to build a human connection, it's your **instinct** that guides you through the subtleties AI can't detect.

Intuition in Decision-Making: Where AI Falls Short

AI is fantastic at offering patterns and predictions based on historical data. But it lacks the ability to make decisions based on **emotional nuance**. It can tell you what worked in the past, but it can't tell you what feels right for the present moment. This is where human intuition reigns supreme.

When crafting content, you may get a perfectly optimized piece of AI-generated copy. But as a Humanizer, you know better. You sense that it doesn't quite **resonate**. Maybe it's missing a personal touch, or perhaps it feels too generic. You trust your gut to make the necessary changes, knowing that this instinctual shift is what will make the content **land emotionally** with the audience.

Make no mistake: this is a huge **strategic advantage**. The brands and creators who can balance data-driven insights with human intuition are the ones who will thrive in a world overwhelmed by automated content.

The Role of Intuition in Creativity

Creativity is, by its very nature, **unpredictable**. It's not something you can program into an algorithm. AI can assist with creative tasks, offering suggestions and even drafting content, but it cannot tap into the **well of human inspiration** that leads to truly groundbreaking ideas.

Human intuition plays a crucial role in **sparking creativity**. It's what tells us to push beyond the expected, to take risks, and to explore the unknown. This creative intuition is the source of innovation, of bold ideas that challenge the status quo. **AI can't take you there.** Only human creativity, driven by instinct and emotion, can lead to those transformative moments where something truly original is born.

Harnessing Intuition: The Humanizer's Edge

As a Humanizer, your greatest advantage is your ability to **trust your instincts**. While others may rely solely on data and automation, you know that the key to meaningful, human-centered content lies in your ability to feel your way through the process. You listen to your gut, you trust your sixth sense, and you know that sometimes the best decisions come from that quiet, inner voice that tells you to go left when everyone else is going right.

Intuition isn't a luxury—it's essential. It's what gives you the edge over AI-driven competitors. It's what allows you to create content that resonates on a deeper level and builds real trust and connection. And it's what will keep the flame of creativity and humanity burning in a world increasingly dominated by automation.

Chapter Eight

THE POWER OF VULNERABILITY IN HUMANIZATION

I f intuition is the compass that guides human connection, **vulnerability** is the openness that allows that connection to happen. In a world where everyone tries to appear perfect—brands included—it's the willingness to show **imperfection** that can truly break through the noise.

Incorporating vulnerability into your copy or content creation process is less about oversharing or revealing weaknesses unnecessarily and much more about **showing humanity** in a way that makes people feel they're engaging with a real person, not just a polished, robotic brand.

Why Vulnerability Resonates

Think about the last time you connected deeply with a piece of content. Chances are, it wasn't because the writer or speaker was presenting themselves as flawless—it was because they allowed their **humanity** to show.

Whether they shared a personal failure, expressed uncertainty, or admitted their struggles, what drew you in was their vulnerability.

Vulnerability is magnetic because it makes others feel safe to be human, too. **Perfection is unrelatable, but imperfection is a shared experience**. And when we share that experience openly, it builds **trust**.

Vulnerability in Copywriting: Why It Matters

When writing copy—especially in a world where AI-generated text is flooding inboxes—vulnerability is your secret weapon. It shows that behind every brand, every product, and every message, there's a **real person**. And in the age of AI, this personal touch is both refreshing and essential.

Here's why vulnerability matters in copywriting:

- **It builds trust**: People trust those who are willing to be honest and open, even about their imperfections.
- **It creates relatability**: Your audience sees themselves in your stories, especially when you're willing to reveal your own struggles or uncertainties.
- **It invites connection**: When we show our vulnerability, we invite others to connect with us on a deeper level.

The Courage to Be Vulnerable

Vulnerability requires **courage**. It means stepping away from the need to appear perfect and embracing the reality that authenticity often involves showing our rough edges. But this is also where the magic happens.

AI cannot be vulnerable. It cannot take the emotional risks that humans can. It cannot show doubt, uncertainty, or personal growth.

As a Humanizer, this is where you shine.

The courage to show vulnerability is what sets you apart from AI-generated content—and it's what will make your messages **memorable**.

How Vulnerability Enhances Intuition

Vulnerability isn't just about exposing your own imperfections. Anyone can do that. It is, at the end of the day, all about **being open to the emotions of others**. When you approach your audience with vulnerability, your **intuition** becomes more finely tuned. You become more sensitive to the unspoken needs, fears, and desires of those you're writing for.

By allowing yourself to be vulnerable in your content, you become more adept at recognizing where your audience feels vulnerable—and this is where true connection happens. It's no longer just about **selling** or **informing**; it's about **understanding and empathizing**.

How to Integrate Vulnerability into Your Copy

Incorporating vulnerability into your content doesn't mean airing your deepest secrets—it's about finding moments where you can **humanize the experience**. Here's how:

1. **Tell personal stories**: Share moments where you didn't have all the answers or struggled with the same challenges your audience faces. Authenticity in storytelling is a powerful tool.
   - *Example*: "When I first started out, I was completely overwhelmed, juggling tasks that felt impossible. It wasn't until I found a system that worked for me that I began to breathe again."

2. **Admit imperfections**: Show that you or your product isn't perfect, but that's okay—because perfection isn't what matters. What matters is the commitment to growth, improvement, and connection.
   o *Example*: "Our service isn't perfect, but neither are we. What we can promise is that we'll always listen, adjust, and improve based on your needs."

3. **Acknowledge your audience's vulnerabilities**: Recognize that your audience has fears, doubts, and struggles. Speak to those feelings openly, creating a space where they feel understood.
   o *Example*: "We know that starting a business is terrifying. The fear of failure, the constant uncertainty, and the weight of responsibility—it's heavy. But you're not alone in this."

4. **Embrace the messiness of the process**: Show that success, growth, or improvement isn't linear—it's a messy process full of missteps, and that's part of the journey.
   o *Example*: "Our journey hasn't been perfect. We've made mistakes, hit roadblocks, and had to pivot more times than we can count. But those moments taught us what really matters—resilience, empathy, and connection."

The Connection Between Vulnerability and Humanization

At its heart, **vulnerability is human**. It's what allows us to connect with one another in ways that go beyond the surface level. It's what makes the content feel **alive**. When we show vulnerability in our writing, we create a space where our audience feels safe to be human, too.

In contrast, AI is **incapable of vulnerability**. It cannot express doubt, fear, or personal growth. It can only mimic confidence, certainty, and structure—missing the complexity of human emotion entirely.

As a Humanizer, your willingness to be vulnerable is what breathes life into your content. It's what allows your audience to trust you, to relate to you, and to believe in what you're offering. Vulnerability may seem like a weakness, but it's actually the **key** to unlocking deeper connections in a world where AI-generated content often feels cold and detached.

The Intersection of Vulnerability, Intuition, and Creativity

When you trust your **intuition** and embrace vulnerability, you allow for the kind of creativity that AI can never replicate. It's in those moments of doubt, uncertainty, or emotional risk-taking that the most **authentic and powerful** ideas emerge.

Vulnerability, intuition, and creativity are all intertwined, forming the foundation of **humanized content** that moves people, inspires action, and builds lasting relationships.

Action Step:

Review a recent piece of sales copy you've written and identify areas where it could be more humanized. Focus on the **empathy, authenticity, vulnerability,** and **emotional connection** in your messaging. Rewrite the copy with these elements and your own intuition in mind and observe the difference in tone and effectiveness.

Chapter Nine

THE POWER OF STORYTELLING IN COPYWRITING

Storytelling is, and always has been, a powerful tool for **human connection**. Before there were marketing strategies, sales funnels, or conversion rates, there were stories—narratives passed down through generations to entertain, inspire, and teach. Today, storytelling remains a cornerstone of communication, especially in **copywriting**.

When you embed storytelling into your copy, you create a **meaningful connection** with your audience that sparks emotion and drives action. And this is something AI, no matter how advanced, struggles to do. AI can string words together, sometimes even elegantly, but it lacks the ability to craft stories that feel **personal, emotional, and real**.

Why Storytelling Works in Copywriting

Let's cut straight to the core: people respond to stories because they speak to our shared human experiences. A good story cuts through the noise and resonates with the reader on an emotional level. To put it bluntly, in copywriting, stories sell.

Storytelling works in this space because:

- **Stories simplify complex ideas**. People don't want a long list of features; they want to know how your product or service is going to fit into their life and make it better.
- **Stories create relatability**. When readers see themselves in the narrative, they're more likely to trust you and your message.
- **Stories trigger emotions**. Whether it's joy, empathy, or urgency, stories pull at heartstrings in ways that straight facts never can.

Your job as a **Humanizer** is to take the ordinary and turn it into something extraordinary by wrapping it in a compelling story. Let's dive into how you can do that effectively.

Why AI Struggles with Storytelling

At first glance, it might seem like AI has mastered storytelling. It can pull together facts, mimic human-like tones, and follow the structure of a classic narrative arc. But here's the reality: AI doesn't tell stories; it assembles them. And that distinction makes all the difference.

AI lacks empathy. It lacks lived experience. It lacks intuition.

It's the difference between reciting lines from a script and truly understanding the meaning behind them. AI can generate words, but it cannot feel. And without feeling, there is no story—at least not one that matters.

The Absence of Empathy

True storytelling begins with empathy—the ability to step into someone else's shoes to understand their deepest fears, most vivid dreams, and most passionate desires. AI doesn't have the capacity for empathy. It can analyze data and detect patterns, but it cannot understand what it feels like to experience joy, loss, frustration, or hope. These emotions are the lifeblood of compelling stories, and they are beyond the reach of any algorithm.

Without empathy, AI's stories are hollow. They may be well-structured, but they lack the beating heart that makes a story resonate. Human stories are all about connection. They're about the unspoken bond that forms between the storyteller and the audience, as they both recognize something familiar in the narrative—a shared emotion, a common struggle.

The Lack of Lived Experience

AI has never lived. It doesn't know what it's like to face adversity, to triumph over challenges, or to find beauty in the mundane. Every great story is rooted in lived experience—whether it's the quiet reflection of a sunrise or the overwhelming relief of an against-all-odds victory.

Human beings tell stories because we've lived them. We've felt the sting of failure, the thrill of success, and the tension of everything in between. AI can't replicate that, no matter how sophisticated it becomes. It doesn't understand the nuances of life's journey, and it certainly doesn't grasp the hard-fought lessons learned along the way.

That's why when AI tries to tell a story, it can feel disconnected from reality. The narrative might make logical sense, but it won't carry the weight of true human experience. It can mimic the structure, but it can't capture the essence. Your audience will detect this.

Human Stories vs. AI Narratives: A Philosophical Defiance

AI-generated content will always be limited by the boundaries of its programming. As it becomes more and more sophisticated, one truth will remain: **it will never truly understand the human condition**. And this is where we, as storytellers, stand our ground.

We must never surrender the art of storytelling to machines.

We cannot let AI define what it means to tell a story.

Our stories are more than just words on a page. They are reflections of our souls, our struggles, our triumphs. They are infused with meaning because our experiences shape them. AI can assemble a narrative, but it cannot tell a story that matters—not in the way a human can.

There is a subtle defiance in being a Humanizer in an age of AI. It's a quiet resistance to the idea that machines can fully replicate the depth and nuance of human emotion. It's a belief that no matter how advanced technology becomes, it will never replace the connection that forms between two people when one shares a story and the other listens.

Storytelling is an act of rebellion. It's a refusal to let algorithms and automation drown out the human voice. It's a declaration that, in a world increasingly driven by data, we still have something invaluable to offer: our humanity.

The Role of the Humanizer: Turning Data into Compelling Stories

This is where you, the Humanizer, come in. AI is not the enemy. It's a tool—a powerful one. But it is just that: a tool. It can gather data, organize information, and even suggest narrative structures. But it's up to you to turn that raw material into something real.

As a Humanizer, you take the threads of data that AI provides and weave them into stories that resonate on a deeply human level. You bring empathy, experience, and intuition to the table—qualities that AI will never possess. You transform facts into feelings insights into inspiration.

YOU are the storyteller. AI can assist, but it is YOUR voice that carries the weight of the narrative. It's your perspective, your understanding of the human condition, that turns a series of events into a compelling journey.

In the end, storytelling creates an emotional experience. It's about taking your audience on a journey that they not only understand but *feel*. AI can assemble facts, but it cannot create the kind of connection that comes from shared human experience.

That's why your role as a Humanizer is so vital. You bridge the gap between data and meaning, between information and emotion. In a world that increasingly relies on AI, you are the one who keeps the heart of storytelling alive.

Here are a few practical tips for incorporating storytelling into your copywriting:

1. **Start with the Audience in Mind**: Always ask yourself, *"What does my audience care about? What are their challenges, and how can I address them in a story?"*

2. **Keep it Relatable**: You don't need to craft an epic tale. Simple, everyday stories often resonate the most because they reflect the reader's own life.

3. **Use Testimonials and Case Studies**: These are real-world stories that show the effectiveness of your product or service. Let your happy customers be the heroes of your narrative.

4. **Don't Overcomplicate It**: A good story doesn't need to be long. It just needs to be **engaging** and **emotionally resonant**.

Key Elements of Storytelling in Copywriting

Every story follows a familiar structure: **a beginning, a middle, and an end**. In copywriting, this structure is often condensed, but the principles remain the same. Here are the essential elements of effective storytelling for your content:

1. The Hook

This is the attention-grabber, the part of the story that pulls your audience in and makes them want to keep reading. It should speak directly to your reader's emotions, curiosity, or needs.

Actionable Example:

- Hook: *"Sarah was exhausted. No matter how hard she worked, her business seemed stuck. But then she discovered a simple shift that changed everything..."*
- Why it works: It taps into a shared pain point—feeling stuck and overworked—and sets up the promise of a solution.

2. The Conflict or Challenge

Great stories always involve some kind of conflict. In the context of copywriting, this is where you address the **problem your audience is facing**. The conflict creates tension, and that tension is what makes the solution you're offering even more appealing.

Actionable Example:

- Conflict: *"Like many small business owners, Sarah struggled with time management. Her to-do list was never-ending, and every day felt like an uphill battle."*
- Why it works: It mirrors the daily struggles of your target audience and sets up the need for your product or service.

3. The Resolution

The resolution is where you introduce your product or service as the solution to the problem. This is where your story transitions from being about your audience's struggle to being about how **you** can help them overcome it.

Actionable Example:

- Resolution: *"That's when Sarah discovered our project management tool. Within weeks, she was organizing her time more efficiently, completing tasks ahead of schedule, and finally finding time to focus on what really mattered—growing her business."*
- Why it works: You're presenting a solution in the form of a relatable story that shows tangible results.

4. The Emotional Payoff

Every story needs an emotional payoff—this is the moment when the reader feels something: hope, relief, excitement, or a sense of possibility. The goal here is to make your audience not just understand the benefits of your product or service but **feel** them.

Actionable Example:

- Payoff: *"Sarah's business is thriving now, and so is she. What once felt impossible is now effortless, and it all started with one simple change."*
- Why it works: The audience can envision themselves in Sarah's shoes, experiencing the same transformation and emotional relief.

Different Types of Stories You Can Use in Your Copy

Not every story has to be a full-blown narrative. Sometimes, short anecdotes or examples work just as well. Let's explore various storytelling techniques that you can apply to bring life, authenticity, and emotional richness to your AI content.

Each technique can be used to enhance the humanization process, ensuring that your AI-generated messages not only communicate effectively but also forge meaningful connections.

Here are a few different storytelling formats you can use in your copy:

The Transformation Story

What it is:

The Transformation Story is the classic "before and after" narrative, showcasing how someone's life or work improved after using a product or service. It paints a clear picture of the benefits through a real or hypothetical example, giving the audience a tangible sense of what's possible.

How to use it:

When presenting your product or service, illustrate the transformation that customers experience. Instead of just talking about features, highlight the emotional and practical shift that occurs—from frustration to relief, from inefficiency to productivity.

Humanization Tip:

To humanize this story, focus on the personal aspects of the transformation. How did the person feel before, and how do they feel now? Emphasize emotions like stress, excitement, or relief, allowing the audience to invest in the story emotionally. Use real-life testimonials or detailed scenarios to make the transformation relatable and compelling.

The "What If" Story

What it is:

The "What If" Story taps into your audience's imagination, helping them visualize an ideal future where their problems are solved and desires are fulfilled. By creating a hypothetical scenario, this storytelling technique appeals to their dreams and aspirations, subtly guiding them to see your product as the bridge to that future.

How to use it:

Use this technique to open possibilities for your audience. Present a series of "what if" questions that align with their pain points and desires making them consider the future they want. Then, position your product or service as the solution that can make that future a reality.

Humanization Tip:

Humanize this story by focusing on the emotional desires that drive the audience—freedom, success, and peace of mind. Avoid being too abstract; ground the "what if" in relatable, day-to-day scenarios that your audience experiences. This way, they can see themselves in the story and feel emotionally connected to the outcome.

The Origin Story

What it is:

An Origin Story tells the backstory of a company, product, or brand. People love hearing how something started, especially when it involves personal struggles, ingenuity, or passion. Sharing this story helps build trust and connection with the audience, making your brand feel more authentic and relatable.

How to use it:

Share your brand's journey—how it began, what challenges you overcame, and the "why" behind what you do. This story gives your audience insight into your mission and values, helping them feel aligned with your purpose. Use it to foster loyalty and trust, especially if your audience cares about the story behind the product as much as the product itself.

Humanization Tip:

To humanize the Origin Story, focus on the personal motivations and emotions involved. What was the emotional driver behind creating your product or starting your company? Sharing personal details, struggles, or moments of inspiration will make the story more relatable and emotionally engaging for your audience.

The Quest Narrative

What it is: The Quest narrative is all about pursuing a goal, often with obstacles along the way. It's driven by a sense of purpose and determination.

How to use it: Frame your content as a journey. In the context of humanizing AI content, the audience's quest could be achieving a personal or professional goal with the help of your product or service. For example, in marketing copy, the quest might be to solve a specific problem or achieve a breakthrough in their business.

Humanization Tip: Include empathetic touchpoints that recognize the reader's struggles along the journey. Highlight the challenges they might face and how your brand or service provides the tools to overcome those obstacles. This adds emotional weight to AI-generated content, turning it into a partnership between you and your audience on their quest.

The Overcoming the Monster Archetype

What it is: In this archetype, the protagonist faces a daunting adversary, which must be confronted and defeated.

How to use it: Identify a common "monster" that your audience faces— this could be anything from a specific pain point, like feeling disconnected from their customers, to larger societal issues, such as impersonal automation.

AI-generated content can be the means by which your audience "slays" this monster, but humanization will provide the emotional context.

Humanization Tip: Paint a vivid picture of the challenges your audience faces, then introduce your solution as the weapon to defeat the monster. Use storytelling to elevate the sense of triumph that comes with victory, allowing readers to invest in the solution emotionally.

The Rags to Riches Story

What it is: This is a classic story of transformation, where the protagonist rises from difficult circumstances to success.

How to use it: For AI content, this technique can be used in case studies or customer testimonials that show how someone went from struggling to thriving after using your product or service. The transformation arc highlights the emotional journey of progress and success.

Humanization Tip: Focus on the personal journey—what fears, frustrations, or challenges did the individual face before they found your solution? How did their life change afterward? AI-generated content can tell a factual story, but the human touch adds emotional depth by celebrating the resilience and triumph of the individual or brand.

The Transformation Arc

What it is: The Transformation Arc centers on internal change, where the protagonist evolves emotionally, intellectually, or spiritually.

How to use it: Apply this in AI content by focusing on how your product or service leads to personal growth or transformation for your audience. This is especially useful for personal development content or brand stories where change is a key theme.

Humanization Tip: Highlight the internal journey. Where did your audience begin, emotionally or mentally, before they encountered your product? What changes occurred? AI can present data or steps in the transformation, but the human touch comes from detailing the personal evolution and emotional revelations along the way.

The Fable or Allegory

What it is: Fables and allegories use symbolic stories to convey a deeper moral or lesson.

How to use it: Humanize your AI content by embedding lessons within metaphorical stories. For instance, if you're discussing the importance of authenticity, you could tell a modern fable where a brand loses its identity by over-automating and is only restored once human values are reintroduced.

Humanization Tip: Use simple, relatable metaphors that align with your audience's experiences. AI-generated content can create the skeleton of the story, but it's the humanized metaphors and moral lessons that will emotionally engage your audience.

The Epiphany Story

What it is: In an Epiphany Story, the protagonist experiences a moment of sudden realization that changes their perspective.

How to use it: Structure your content around the "aha!" moment. This could be when your audience realizes they've been missing a key strategy, insight, or tool that will transform their work or lives. For example, if your AI tool helps businesses communicate more effectively, the epiphany might be when a business owner realizes their messaging lacked personalization until now.

Humanization Tip: Focus on the emotions tied to the realization. AI can describe the rational elements of the epiphany, but you need to convey the sense of clarity, relief, or excitement that accompanies it. This emotional layering creates a powerful connection with your reader.

Nested or Frame Stories

What it is: A Nested or Frame Story is a story within a story, where the outer narrative sets the context for the inner one.

How to use it: Use this technique to tell layered stories about your brand, product, or customers. Start with a broad narrative (e.g., the importance of humanizing AI content), and then embed smaller, specific stories of success or challenges within that framework.

Humanization Tip: The outer story provides the context or theme, while the inner stories give concrete examples. AI can generate the structure, but humanizing means adding emotional resonance to each individual's journey, making it relatable to your audience.

The Conflict and Resolution Narrative

What it is: This narrative revolves around a conflict that must be resolved, usually involving tension or a challenge that builds throughout the story.

How to use it: Present a conflict that your audience faces (e.g., poor customer engagement, impersonal messaging), and show how the conflict is resolved through your product, service, or approach. The key is in showing how human oversight and intuition help resolve the issues that AI alone cannot fix.

Humanization Tip: Draw out the emotional stakes of the conflict. What's at risk for your audience? Use empathy to connect with their fears or frustrations, and then offer your solution as a way to relieve that tension. AI can provide a logical resolution, but it's the human touch that adds emotional relief.

The Unexpected Twist

What it is: A story with an unexpected twist subverts the audience's expectations, often leading to a surprising or unconventional outcome.

How to use it: You can use this technique to engage your audience by setting up an anticipated scenario and then flipping the narrative. For example, build up a conventional idea of how AI works in content creation, then reveal that true success comes from humanization and not automation alone.

Humanization Tip: Use humor, surprise, or an emotional pivot to keep the audience engaged. AI can help with the setup and execution, but the emotional impact of the twist will come from how well you understand and play with your audience's expectations.

The Journey of Many

What it is: This narrative follows multiple protagonists, each with their own journey, and brings them together toward a common conclusion.

How to use it: In AI content, this can be used to showcase different personas or customer journeys that lead to the same ultimate goal—success, growth, or fulfillment. You can show how various people, with their unique perspectives and challenges, have found success through your product or service.

Humanization Tip: Each journey should feel personal and emotionally resonant. AI can generate the structure of multiple stories, but humanization happens when you dig into the specific emotional experiences of each person. How did their journey start? What challenges were unique to them? By humanizing each character, you provide a more complete and emotionally satisfying narrative.

These storytelling techniques offer a wealth of tools to humanize AI-generated content. By blending AI's efficiency with the emotional depth of storytelling, you create content that resonates on a deeper, more meaningful level.

Whether you're framing a customer success story, crafting a brand narrative, or creating marketing copy, these storytelling frameworks ensure that your audience feels seen, heard, and emotionally connected.

Humanizing The Hero's Journey

The **Hero's Journey** is a narrative structure that dates back to ancient storytelling and remains relevant today. It's used in everything from movies to books to advertising.

In copywriting, the Hero's Journey can be an incredibly powerful tool to draw your audience in by positioning **them** as the hero and **your product or service** as the guide that helps them overcome challenges.

Here's how the Hero's Journey breaks down in a **copywriting context**:

1. The Ordinary World

This is where you describe the current state of your audience's world. It's the day-to-day reality they're experiencing, which includes their pain points, struggles, and frustrations.

Example:

- *"Running a business isn't easy. You're juggling too many tasks, your to-do list never seems to end, and there's always another challenge waiting around the corner."*

2. The Call to Adventure

The "call to adventure" is the moment when the hero (your customer) realizes that they need to change or find a solution to their problem. In copywriting, this is where you position your product or service as the answer to their challenges.

Example:

- *"But what if there was a way to simplify everything? What if you could finally find a solution that would give you back your time, reduce stress, and help you focus on what truly matters?"*

3. The Guide (Your Product or Service)

In the Hero's Journey, the hero meets a guide who offers them the tools or wisdom they need to succeed. In copywriting, your business or product is the guide that helps the hero (your audience) on their journey.

Example:

- *"That's where our software comes in. We've helped thousands of business owners like you take control of their workload, streamline their operations, and focus on growth."*

4. The Transformation

This is the "aha" moment when the hero sees the benefits of using your product or service. It's where the transformation begins, and the results become clear.

Example:

- *"With our software, you'll go from feeling overwhelmed and overworked to feeling empowered, efficient, and back in control. Your business will run like clockwork, and you'll have more time for the things that matter most."*

5. The Return (The New Normal)

In the final stage of the Hero's Journey, the hero returns to their world, transformed by their experience. In copywriting, this is where you show your audience the lasting impact of using your product or service.

Example:

- *"Now, you can spend less time managing tasks and more time growing your business and enjoying your life. The stress is gone, and you're finally in control of your day-to-day operations."*

Applying the Hero's Journey in Different Types of Content

The beauty of the Hero's Journey is that it can be applied across various forms of content—not just in your direct copy but also in **About pages, bios for podcasts, social media posts**, and more.

Here's how you can humanize different types of content using storytelling.

1. Writing an Engaging About Page

Your **About page** is one of the most important pieces of content on your website. It's where potential customers learn who you are, what you stand for, and why they should trust you. Instead of writing a dry, third-person bio, turn your About page into a **narrative** that guides the reader through your journey.

Here's how to apply the Hero's Journey to an About page:

- **Ordinary World**: Where did your business start? What challenges did you face? What inspired you to create your product or service?
- **Call to Adventure**: What was the turning point that made you realize you had to start this business? What problem were you trying to solve?
- **Guide**: What makes your product or service unique? How does it guide your customers through their own challenges?
- **Transformation**: What results have you achieved, and how has your business grown? What impact has your business had on your customers?

Example:

"Back in 2015, I was working 60-hour weeks in corporate marketing, feeling burnt out and unfulfilled. I knew there had to be a better way to help small businesses thrive without the overwhelmed. That's why I started [Your Business], a company dedicated to helping entrepreneurs simplify their marketing and find more freedom in their lives."

2. Crafting Bios for Podcasts

When you're asked to submit a **bio for a podcast**, it's tempting to list your credentials and call it a day. But a more human approach is to weave your bio into a **mini-story** that highlights your personal journey and connects with the podcast audience.

Instead of just listing your accomplishments, share:

- What sparked your journey into your field?
- What challenges did you overcome?
- How you're making a difference in the industry today.

Example:

"After spending years working in traditional marketing, I realized that the industry was becoming too robotic and disconnected. I wanted to bring the human element back into business, so I founded [Your Company], where we help businesses infuse empathy and authenticity into their copy and content."

3. Social Media Posts

Social media is the perfect place to experiment with **storytelling** in short bursts. Rather than posting standard updates, share stories that your audience can relate to. You can follow the Hero's Journey in mini-format to keep posts engaging.

Example:

"Feeling overwhelmed by your daily to-do list? That was me a year ago, juggling way too many projects and never feeling caught up. Then, I discovered a new approach that helped me take control of my time and my business. Here's how you can do the same…"

4. Case Studies

When writing **case studies**, think of your customer as the hero of the story. Walk your audience through the challenge your customer faced, how your product or service acted as the guide, and the transformation that followed.

Example:

"When Jen, a small business owner, first came to us, she was struggling with managing her team's workload. We worked with her to implement our project management software, and within three months, her productivity had increased by 40%. Now, Jen is thriving, and so is her team."

Other Ways Storytelling Can Humanize Your Copy

Humanizing your copy through storytelling is one of the most powerful ways to engage and connect with your audience. Storytelling allows you to transcend traditional marketing tactics by weaving emotional and relatable narratives into your content.

Here are a few ways to incorporate humanized storytelling into various aspects of your copywriting:

1. Email Campaigns: From Promotion to Journey

Emails are a prime space for humanized storytelling because they provide a direct line to your audience's inbox. Instead of sending generic promotional emails that focus solely on discounts or features, use storytelling to guide your audience through a personal journey of discovery.

How to Apply It:

- **Customer Success Story**: Share a story about how one of your customers overcame a major challenge by using your product or service. Rather than just listing features, show the emotional transformation—from frustration to relief—and how your product was a key part of their success.

- **Your Brand's Origin Story**: Take your audience behind the scenes, letting them in on why your company started and the mission driving you forward. This adds a personal layer to your communications, giving your readers a reason to invest in your brand emotionally.

Example:

"Meet Sarah, a small business owner who was overwhelmed with managing her daily operations. She was working long hours, missing family dinners, and felt like she was failing to find balance. That was until she discovered [Your Product], which transformed how she managed her time. Now, Sarah can leave work at a reasonable hour and finally enjoy the life she worked so hard to build. Here's how you can experience the same..."

2. Sales Pages: Transforming the Customer's Journey

A great sales page doesn't just list benefits or describe features. It tells a compelling story about how your product or service transforms the lives of your customers. Storytelling on a sales page highlights the emotional journey a customer undergoes—from frustration and uncertainty to success and fulfillment.

How to Apply It:

- **Customer-Centric Story**: Focus on a real or hypothetical customer journey where the problem they face is one your audience can relate to. Show how they felt before discovering your product, the turning point when they found your solution, and the success they achieved afterward.

- **Story as a Solution**: Instead of simply explaining the product, use a story to showcase how it acts as the "hero" or "guide" in helping your audience achieve their desired outcome.

Example:

"Imagine feeling stuck—every project taking twice as long, every deadline looming over your head. That's exactly how John felt before he discovered [Your Product]. Within days of implementing it, his productivity skyrocketed, his stress levels dropped, and he was back to running his business with ease. Here's how [Your Product] can help you do the same..."

3. Product Descriptions: The Story Behind the Solution

Even something as seemingly straightforward as a product description can benefit from storytelling. Rather than simply stating technical specs, weave a narrative that conveys the human element behind the product. Share why it was created, the problem it solves, or the personal stories of the people who have benefited from it.

How to Apply It:

- **Creator Story**: Share the story of how your product came to be—what inspired its creation and what problem it set out to solve. This gives readers insight into the heart of the product.

- **Customer Testimonial Story**: Add depth to a product description by embedding a customer testimonial that tells a short story of transformation. Focus on the emotions the customer experienced before and after using your product.

Example:

"[Your Product] wasn't just built to improve efficiency—it was created out of necessity. Our founder, Jane, struggled for years with outdated systems that slowed down her business. After countless sleepless nights and frustrations, she decided to create a solution that would revolutionize the way teams work. Today, [Your Product] helps thousands of businesses save time and stay ahead of the curve."

4. Blog Posts: Weaving Personal Narratives

Blogs offer an excellent platform for diving deeper into storytelling. Whether you're sharing industry insights, educational content, or updates, incorporating personal or customer stories into blog posts makes them more engaging and memorable. Use blog storytelling to create an emotional connection that keeps readers coming back.

How to Apply It:

- **Personal Experiences**: Weave your own experiences and challenges into the narrative of your blog posts. When discussing a solution, start with a relatable problem that you or someone else has faced. This not only humanizes your content but also makes it more relatable and actionable.

- **Success Stories**: Share success stories of real clients, explaining how your product or service helped them overcome obstacles. Let your blog readers feel like they're part of a community of people finding solutions to similar problems.

Example:

"I remember the first time I faced burnout as a freelance writer. I had taken on too many projects, lost my passion, and started questioning my future. That's when I discovered the importance of setting boundaries and focusing on quality over quantity. Today, I teach others how to avoid the same mistakes I made using these five simple principles..."

5. Social Media Posts: Micro-Storytelling

With limited characters, social media posts need to be sharp, engaging, and emotionally resonant rather than just broadcasting information and sharing micro-stories that draw readers in and make them care.

How to Apply It:

- **Customer Highlights**: Share quick customer success stories or "day in the life" narratives that show how your product impacts people's lives. A few short sentences and an accompanying image can convey a powerful emotional message.
- **Behind-the-Scenes Stories:** Give your audience a glimpse into your daily life or the creative process behind your product. Sharing stories of the hard work, passion, and commitment behind your brand builds trust and relatability.

Example:

"Ever feel like you're drowning in endless tasks? That's exactly how Emily felt before she found our time management app. Now, she's back to enjoying her weekends. Ready to take back your time? Start your free trial today."

6. Video Scripts: Bringing Stories to Life

Video is a powerful storytelling medium. Whether it's a short explainer video, a testimonial, or a brand story, incorporating narrative elements into your video scripts can make them more engaging and emotionally resonant.

How to Apply It:

- **Testimonial Stories**: Have customers share their journey in their own words, focusing on the emotional transformation they experienced.
- **Brand Story Videos**: Create a video that tells the story of your brand, your mission, and how your product or service changes lives. Use real-life examples and emotions to make it relatable.

Example:

"Meet James. Three years ago, he was drowning in paperwork, unable to focus on growing his business. After trying every tool on the market, he almost gave up. That's when he found [Your Product], and his life changed. Now, James runs his business efficiently and has the freedom to focus on what matters most. Here's how [Your Product] made the difference..."

Storytelling humanizes your brand and deepens the emotional connection with your audience. Whether in emails, sales pages, product descriptions, or even social media, adding storytelling elements makes your content more relatable, memorable, and effective.

The key is to focus on the human experience—the challenges, transformations, and emotions that your audience can connect with.

Storytelling is an essential tool in **humanizing content,** but it's only one part of the bigger picture. In the next chapter, we'll dive into the importance of **empathy** and how you can use it to create content that not only resonates but builds trust and loyalty with your audience.

Stories are how we make sense of the world, and they are how we connect with one another. As a Humanizer, your ability to tell stories that evoke emotion and create connection will set you apart in the crowded world of AI-driven content. Let your stories be the key that unlocks those deeper connections.

Action Step:
Identify one area of your business or content strategy where you can better balance your own story with AI and humanization. Take a concrete step to bring more human insight into that area, whether it's rewriting your about page, your bio, or a story in one of your sales emails, and start being mindful of how you add personal stories to your marketing or customer interactions.

Chapter Ten

MASTERING EMPATHY IN CONTENT CREATION

mpathy is a Humanizer's superpower. It's the one thing AI will never have, no matter how sophisticated the technology becomes. Empathy allows us to understand and connect with others on a deeply emotional level. And in the world of content creation, this makes all the difference.

Empathy is non-negotiable. If you're not writing with empathy, you're just another voice lost in the noise—a cold, robotic echo of AI-generated content that lacks the very thing people crave: connection. The last thing your audience wants is another sales pitch; they want to be seen, heard and understood.

Let me be clear: AI can't do this. It can provide data, structure, and even simulate tone, but it will never be able to write from the heart. It's your job, as a Humanizer, to bring that empathy into your writing—to turn data into emotion and create content that resonates far beyond the superficial.

Why Empathy is Non-Negotiable in Humanized Content

At its core, empathy is about going deeper—deeper than just your audience's surface-level needs or demographics. It's about understanding their emotions, their struggles, and their desires. It's about walking in their shoes and asking:

- What are they feeling right now?
- What keeps them up at night?
- What do they truly need—not just what they *say* they need?

When you answer these questions, you stop being just another marketer or copywriter. You become a guide, a trusted ally in their journey. You create messages that cut through the clutter, not because they're clever or optimized for SEO, but because they're human. In a world that's drowning in content, this is your lifeline to stand out.

The Problem with AI: It Lacks Empathy

Let's face it: empathy isn't something you can fake. You can't manufacture it with an algorithm or program it into AI. Empathy is real—it's felt. And **your audience can sense when it's missing**. They can smell a phony a mile away.

AI may be able to write grammatically flawless copy, but without empathy, it's just that: flawless. It's *too* perfect. It's missing the messiness, the emotion, the *humanness* that makes writing meaningful. Your job is to inject that emotion, to turn the flawless into something *real*.

Can AI Really Humanize Content?

We're being flooded with AI tools claiming to "humanize" content, so it's pretty tempting to get swept up in the promises of faster, smarter, and more efficient communication. These algorithms can analyze data, predict sentiment, and even string together words that resemble human emotion. It's downright chilling when you think about it.

But for all its computational power, AI remains a reflection of patterns—**an echo of human inputs**, not the source.

True humanization isn't just about crafting sentences that trigger emotions; it's about understanding the raw, unfiltered human experience. It's about the unspoken moments, the quiet hesitations, and the deep connections we forge with others through shared vulnerability. AI can simulate, but it cannot feel.

It can mimic, but it cannot intuit. It can follow the formula, but it cannot rewrite it with the passion of lived experience.

The essence of humanization—what makes content truly resonate—comes from a place AI will never reach. It comes from our imperfections, our stories, our ability to look beyond data and see the beating heart in the messiness of human life.

While AI tools can assist in shaping content, they will never replace the intangible spark that only a human can provide. In a world rushing toward automation, it's **our very humanness** that will always stand tall, defying the notion that a machine can capture what it means to be alive.

Here's why AI, despite its advanced capabilities, can't fully humanize content:

1. **AI Mimics But Doesn't Experience**: AI can generate content that appears human, but it does so by analyzing patterns, data, and algorithms. It doesn't actually **feel** empathy, joy, or frustration. When humans write content, we pull from our personal experiences and emotions, giving our words an emotional depth that AI simply can't replicate.

2. **Subtlety and Emotional Nuance**: AI is adept at processing large amounts of data and generating text based on that data, but it lacks the ability to understand the subtle, often unspoken emotions behind a message. A human writer can pick up on the smallest emotional cues, adjusting tone and phrasing to meet the reader where they are emotionally.

3. **Understanding Context**: AI relies on data and pre-existing templates to craft messages. While this works for technical copy or surface-level content, it struggles when context, subtext, or deeper emotional layers are required. Empathy in content creation goes beyond what can be analyzed or predicted by a machine—it requires an **emotional intelligence** that AI simply doesn't possess.

Bottom Line: Human Touch Is Irreplaceable

The fact is, while AI can generate content more efficiently and at scale, the **human touch** is irreplaceable when it comes to creating truly meaningful and empathetic content. As we navigate the world of content creation, the goal isn't to replace human writers with AI but to use AI as a **tool** that supports the creative process.

The emotional depth, subtlety, and nuance required for real empathy can only come from human insight.

How to Write with Empathy: A Defiant Approach

Empathy will never come from a checklist. It comes from listening, observing, and putting yourself in your audience's shoes. Here's how to approach empathy in a way that sets you apart.

1. Start with Radical Audience Research

Empathy begins with knowing your audience better than they know themselves. Forget surface-level demographics. Go deeper. What motivates them? What keeps them up at night? What are their fears, dreams, and aspirations?

Example:

- Don't write for "entrepreneurs." Write for the *overwhelmed entrepreneur*—the one who's drowning in their to-do list and feels like they're one step away from burning out.
- Don't write for "new moms." Write for the *exhausted new mom* who's trying to juggle sleepless nights, a demanding job, and the guilt of not being "enough."

Your audience doesn't want generic content. They want to know that you *get* them. And that only happens when you dig deep and understand their emotional landscape.

2. Call Out Their Pain Points—Don't Sugarcoat It

If you want to write with empathy, stop dancing around the real issues. Acknowledge the pain your audience is feeling. Don't be afraid to say, "Yeah, this sucks, and I get it."

Example:

- Instead of saying, "We understand your challenges," say, "We know how frustrating it is to pour your heart into creating content only to hear crickets. You've done the research, put in the effort, and still, it feels like no one's listening."

When you acknowledge their pain, you create an instant emotional connection. You're no longer just selling a product or service—you're offering a solution to a real human problem.

3. Ditch the Corporate Speak: Write Like a Human

Empathy isn't communicated through stiff, formal language. You're not a robot, and neither is your audience. Write like you're talking to a friend—someone you care about.

Example:

- Instead of saying, "Our product will help optimize your workflow," try, "We know you're juggling a million things right now. We're here to help you take back control of your time and your sanity."

The more conversational your tone, the more human your message feels. It's like having a real conversation, not just delivering a polished pitch.

4. Solve Their Problems with Empathy

When you offer a solution, don't just focus on the product—focus on *why* that product matters to them. Show that you understand the emotional journey they're on.

Example:

- "We created this tool because we've been where you are. We know the stress of trying to do it all, and we wanted to build something that gives you the freedom to focus on what really matters."

You're not there to merely solve a problem; you're showing them that you care about their well-being. That's empathy in action.

5. Tell Real Stories that Resonate

As we discussed in the previous chapter, nothing builds empathy faster than storytelling. Use real-world examples and case studies to show your audience that they're not alone—that you've helped others just like them.

Example:

- "When Sarah first came to us, she was on the verge of burnout. She felt like no matter how hard she worked, she was always falling behind. Within just a few weeks of using our service, Sarah had taken control of her time, regained her energy, and found the balance she thought was impossible."

This testimonial is actually a story of transformation. And stories, when told with empathy, are one of the most powerful tools in your content creation arsenal.

6. Ask Open-Ended Questions

Empathy is a conversation. Ask your audience open-ended questions that invite them to reflect on their own experiences.

Example:

- "What would your day look like if you didn't have to spend hours putting out fires? What if you had more time for the things that matter most?"

These questions don't just get your audience thinking—they get them *feeling*. And once they start feeling, they're more likely to engage with your message.

Empathy: The Foundation of Trust and Loyalty

Here's the truth: empathy builds trust. And trust builds loyalty. When your audience feels like you truly understand them—when they feel seen, heard, and valued—they're not just going to buy from you once. They're going to stick around. They're going to tell their friends. They're going to become advocates for your brand.

Empathy isn't limited to long-form blog posts or heartfelt emails. It should be woven into every piece of content you create—from a short social media post to a hard-hitting ad campaign.

1. Social Media Posts:

- "We get it—there's a lot on your plate right now. What's your biggest challenge when it comes to managing your workload? Let's figure it out together."

2. Email Campaigns:

- "Your inbox is probably overflowing right now, so we'll keep this short. How can we help you take a load off and simplify your day?"

3. Ad Copy:

- "Tired of feeling like you're always running to catch up? We get it. Our tool is here to help you take control so you can breathe a little easier."

The Defiant Power of Empathy

In a world obsessed with speed, automation, and efficiency, empathy is an act of defiance.

It's a refusal to treat people like numbers on a screen or clicks in a funnel.

It's a declaration that human connection still matters—that in the age of AI, the brands that will thrive are the ones that refuse to abandon their humanity.

It's what makes your content resonate, your brand memorable, and your audience loyal.

Empathy is the key to standing out in a sea of automated, soulless content. It's the fire that keeps your message burning long after the algorithm forgets it.

With AI cranking out content at lightning speed, having empathy in your toolbox is your edge. It's the difference between being heard and being ignored. The more you lean into empathy, the more you'll connect with your audience—and the more trust, loyalty, and success you'll build.

Action Step:

Practice empathy in your next piece of content. Before you write, take a moment to put yourself in your audience's shoes. Write down what they're feeling, what they need, and how your message can address those needs. Use this insight to shape your content from a place of understanding.

Chapter Eleven

APPLYING HUMANIZATION IN SALES COPYWRITING

S ales copywriting is an art form. It's about more than just crafting clever headlines or listing product benefits—it's about making a genuine **connection** with your audience and taking them by the hand toward a decision that feels right for them.

In the age of AI, this has become even more important. AI can churn out endless streams of sales copy, but what it lacks is the ability to *humanize* the sales process—something only you, as a **Humanizer**, can do.

In this chapter, we'll explore how to **apply humanization techniques** in your sales copy so that it feels authentic, empathetic, and, most importantly, compelling.

Why Sales Copy Needs Humanization

At its core, sales copy is about persuading someone to take action—whether it's to make a purchase, sign up for a service, or simply click through to learn more. But here's the thing: **people don't like to be sold to.** They don't want to feel like they're being manipulated or pressured into making a decision.

This is where **humanized sales copy** comes into play. By focusing on the **needs, emotions, and motivations** of your audience, you can create sales messages that don't feel like a hard sell. Instead, they feel like a conversation—a genuine offer to solve a problem or improve their life.

How to Humanize Sales Copy: Key Techniques

Humanized sales copy is about more than just writing with empathy. It's about creating an experience that makes your audience feel understood, respected, and excited to take the next step. Here's how to make that happen.

1. Lead with Empathy, Not Features

One of the most common mistakes in sales copywriting is leading with a list of features. While it's important to highlight what your product or service can do, that's not where the emotional connection happens. To humanize your sales copy, you need to start by addressing the **emotional needs** of your audience.

Example:

- AI-driven sales copy might say: *"Our software offers 24/7 customer support, cloud-based storage, and real-time analytics."*

- Humanized version: *"We understand how stressful it can be to manage your business when things go wrong after hours. That's why we offer 24/7 support, so you never have to worry about being left in the dark."*

By leading with empathy and focusing on the emotional why, you're creating a deeper connection from the very beginning.

2. Address Pain Points, but Offer Hope

It's important to acknowledge your audience's pain points in sales copy, but equally important is offering them **hope**.

When you dwell too much on the problem, you risk creating anxiety. Instead, aim to balance the acknowledgment of the pain point with a **positive outcome** that your product or service can provide.

Example:

- Pain point: *"We know how overwhelming it is to juggle endless tasks and deadlines and how frustrating it is to feel like you're never making progress."*
- Hope: *"But it doesn't have to be that way. With our solution, you can take back control of your schedule and finally focus on what matters most."*

This approach shows empathy for the audience's struggles while presenting your product as the solution that will improve their lives.

3. Use Testimonials and Social Proof to Build Trust

One of the most powerful ways to humanize your sales copy is by incorporating **real customer stories** and testimonials. Social proof adds credibility to your claims and helps potential customers see how your product or service has helped others just like them.

Example:

- AI copy might say: *"Over 10,000 businesses have used our service."*
- Humanized version: *"Jen, a small business owner like you, was overwhelmed by the constant demands of running her company. After using our service, she streamlined her operations, gained more free time, and saw her business thrive."*

This approach makes the customer the hero of the story, which is far more relatable and persuasive than abstract statistics.

4. Focus on the Emotional Benefits, Not Just the Rational Ones

AI-generated sales copy tends to focus heavily on **rational benefits**—efficiency, productivity, and cost savings. While these are important, they don't create an emotional connection. Humanized sales copy digs deeper and highlights the **emotional benefits** that come with the decision to buy.

Example:

- AI copy: *"Our software helps you save time and increase productivity."*
- Humanized version: *"Imagine finishing your workday with time to spare—so you can spend more time with your family, pursue your passions, or simply relax. That's what our software can do for you."*

By focusing on how your product will **improve your audience's life**, you make the benefits feel more tangible and desirable.

5. Create a Sense of Belonging

People don't just want to buy products or services—they want to feel like they're part of something bigger. Whether it's a movement, a community, or a shared mission, humanized sales copy taps into this desire for belonging.

Example:

- AI copy: *"Our membership program offers exclusive discounts and resources."*
- Humanized version: *"When you join our membership program, you're not just gaining access to discounts—you're joining a community of like-minded people who are passionate about achieving more and supporting each other along the way."*

This approach creates an emotional connection by offering a **sense of community** and shared goals.

Common Pitfalls to Avoid in Sales Copywriting

While humanizing sales copy is about creating connection, there are a few common pitfalls to avoid:

1. Being Too Pushy

Nobody likes a hard sell. If your sales copy feels too aggressive or manipulative, you'll push potential customers away. Instead, focus on **guiding** your audience toward a decision that feels natural and aligned with their needs.

2. Overloading with Features

While it's tempting to highlight every feature of your product, this can overwhelm the reader and dilute the emotional message. Stick to the most relevant features and **connect them to the emotional benefits.**

3. Using Jargon

Sales copy filled with jargon or overly technical language creates a barrier between you and your audience. Keep your language simple, clear, and conversational to maintain that human connection.

The Power of a Humanized Call to Action

The **Call to Action (CTA)** is one of the most important parts of any sales copy. It's the moment when you ask your audience to take the next step. To humanize your CTA, avoid overly formal or transactional language like "Buy now" or "Sign up today." Instead, craft a CTA that feels personal and connected to the emotional journey you've led your audience through.

Actionable Example:

- AI copy: *"Sign up for our newsletter."*
- Humanized version: *"Let's stay in touch—sign up for weekly tips and insights that will help you take your business to the next level."*

This approach feels more like an invitation to continue a conversation rather than a demand to take action.

Next Steps

Humanizing your sales copy isn't just about writing with empathy—it's about creating a sales experience that feels **personal, authentic, and**

emotionally resonant. When you humanize the sales process, you not only increase the chances of conversion, but you also build long-term trust and loyalty with your audience.

The Humanizers' Practical Guide to Humanizing AI-Generated Copy

Humanizing content is a process, one that you can follow to take AI-generated copy and turn it into something that feels personal, authentic, and emotionally resonant.

Here's the step-by-step method for transforming AI-generated content into truly *humanized* copy:

Step 1: Generate AI Content

Start by generating the initial draft using an AI tool. This could be for a promotional email, sales letter, blog post, or even social media content.

Prompt Example:

"Write a promotional email about a productivity tool that helps people manage their time better. Include the features of the tool and call to action."

Once the AI generates the content, **copy and paste** the output into a Word or Google document for the next step.

Step 2: Read It Like Your Audience

Take a moment to **put yourself in the shoes of your audience**. Read through the AI-generated copy and ask yourself these key questions:

- Does this feel like a conversation, or does it sound robotic?
- Do the emotions resonate with me as a reader?

- Does the language feel personal, or does it seem too formal and generic?

What to Look For:

- **Red Flags**: Stiff, overly formal language or phrases that feel repetitive and lack personality.
- **Opportunities**: Where can you infuse more empathy? Where can you add personal touches or stories?

Step 3: Identify the Core Message

Next, **identify the core message** of the content. What is the most important thing you want the audience to walk away with?

This is the time to **simplify**. Look for unnecessary jargon or overcomplicated sentences. AI-generated content often over-explains. Strip it back to **one core idea** or **emotional hook**.

Core Message Example:

AI might write: "Our productivity tool offers streamlined efficiency with automated task management and time-tracking capabilities."

Simplified Humanized Version:

"We help you regain control of your day so you can focus on what truly matters."

Step 4: Add Empathy & Emotional Language

Now, it's time to **inject empathy**. Think about your audience's emotional state—what are they feeling, and how can you address their struggles? AI lacks emotional intuition, so this is where **you bring in the human touch**.

Example:

AI might write:

"With our tool, you can improve efficiency and time management."

Humanized rewrite:

"We understand how stressful it can be to feel like the day's slipping away. That's why we created a tool to help you take control of your time and finally breathe easier."

Ask yourself:

- How would I say this if I were speaking directly to a friend or colleague?
- Am I showing that I genuinely care about their pain points and challenges?

Step 5: Add Storytelling Elements

People don't connect with facts alone—they connect with **stories**. A simple anecdote or relatable narrative can turn bland AI content into something memorable.

Example:

AI might write:

"This tool will help streamline your workflow."

Humanized version with storytelling:

"Meet Sarah. Like many of us, she was drowning in to-do lists and endless tasks. After trying our tool, she now ends her day feeling accomplished and finally has time to spend with her family."

Your Turn: Add a quick **customer story** or personal experience to give your content emotional weight.

Step 6: Personalize the Tone

Go through the AI-generated copy and adjust the tone. Make it feel **conversational and approachable**. Avoid corporate speak or phrases that feel generic or stiff.

Example:

AI might write:

"Our service increases productivity by automating tasks."

Humanized version:

"We're here to help you stop feeling overwhelmed by your to-do list. Let's make your day easier so you can focus on what matters."

Ask yourself:

- Is this how I'd talk to a friend or colleague?
- Does this feel like a real conversation, or does it sound overly formal?

Step 7: Add a Call to Action (CTA)

When wrapping up, your **call to action** shouldn't feel like a hard sell. It should be an invitation to take action based on the emotional journey you've just walked them through.

AI-generated CTA:

"Click here to buy our product now."

Humanized CTA:

"We know you're ready for a change. Click here to see how our tool can help you get your time—and your life—back on track."

You're **inviting them** to take action because you've already built trust and emotional connection through the previous steps.

Step 8: Read It Aloud

Before finalizing, **read the content aloud**. This will help you hear whether it flows naturally or still sounds stiff.

Ask yourself:

- Does this sound like me?
- Does it feel conversational and engaging, or does it still sound mechanical?

If anything feels off, go back and tweak the language until it feels **real and personal**.

Step 9: Test & Get Feedback

Send out your newly humanized content and **track engagement**. How are people responding?

Do you notice more interaction, deeper connections, or positive feedback?

If possible, **get direct feedback** from people who resonate with your content. Ask them:

- Does this content feel personal to you?
- Do you feel like it addresses your real challenges?

This feedback will help refine your humanizing process over time.

Humanization Secrets No One Is Talking About

While AI can deliver content that's technically correct and even creative, it often misses the heart of what connects us as people. The subtle elements that give the language its depth and nuance—the things that make us laugh, feel understood, or transported to another place—are what humanize the message. These are the elements that make people say, "This speaks to me," instead of, "This sounds like a robot."

What many don't realize is that humanization is not just about inserting emotions or personality into content. It's about capturing the essence of what makes us human—our quirks, our shared experiences, and our ability to see ourselves in the stories we tell.

The good news is that there are several powerful yet often overlooked techniques that anyone can use to infuse more humanity into their writing, presentations, and conversations.

These are the humanization secrets no one is talking about—hidden in plain sight but highly effective in making your communication resonate on a deeper level. Let's explore how to use idioms, colloquialisms, metaphors, and more to bring your content to life in ways that AI, no matter how advanced, just can't replicate.

1. **Idioms and Colloquialisms:**
   Using idioms and colloquial phrases adds an authentic, conversational tone that resonates with people on a personal level. It bridges the gap between formal content and the everyday language people use, making communication feel more human. For example, saying "a penny for your thoughts" instead of "What do you think?" immediately brings a sense of warmth and familiarity.

2. **Metaphors and Analogies:**

   Metaphors and analogies make complex ideas more digestible by connecting them to familiar concepts. They create vivid mental images, triggering emotional responses and helping people grasp abstract or challenging topics. For instance, describing AI as "the co-pilot to your creativity" evokes an image of partnership and support rather than technological complexity.

3. **Universal Experiences:**

   Referencing shared human experiences (e.g., childhood memories, waiting in line, finding a quiet moment to reflect) taps into emotions and memories that almost everyone can relate to. This creates a strong connection because it reminds people of their own lives and experiences, making the message feel deeply personal.

4. **Sensory Language:**

   Engaging the senses—sight, sound, touch, taste, and smell—adds texture to the writing. Describing something as "the crisp crunch of autumn leaves underfoot" or "the rich, warm aroma of freshly brewed coffee" invites the reader to experience the message on a sensory level, which humanizes the content and makes it more vivid.

5. **Cultural References and Pop Culture:**

   When used carefully, pop culture references and cultural touchstones can spark recognition and connection. Whether it's a quote from a classic movie or a reference to a trending meme, this approach instantly signals that the message is in tune with the audience's world, adding a layer of relatability.

6. **Emotional Nuance and Imperfection:**

   Rather than presenting everything as polished or perfect, acknowledging vulnerability and imperfections is a powerful humanization tool. Saying things like "I've struggled with this too" or sharing a moment of failure or self-doubt creates empathy and authenticity, allowing the audience to feel more connected to the speaker or writer.

7. **Localized Language and Context:**

   Using specific regional references or cultural nuances that reflect the audience's background (e.g., mentioning local landmarks, foods, or traditions) can immediately create a sense of belonging. It shows that the content creator understands the audience's unique context, making communication more intimate.

8. **Inclusive and Flexible Language:**

   Incorporating gender-neutral, culturally sensitive, or inclusive language makes the message feel relevant to a wider audience. It reflects a sensitivity to diversity, reinforcing the idea that communication values each individual as part of a larger human family.

9. **Storytelling Through Dialogue:**

   Crafting short, conversational dialogues within content can make it feel like a real, relatable story rather than a distant monologue. For example, instead of just stating facts, weaving in a back-and-forth conversation between characters creates a more engaging human dynamic.

10. **Humor and Playfulness:**

Humor lightens the tone and invites a sense of connection through laughter. Whether it's a light-hearted joke, a playful pun, or a self-deprecating comment, humor brings down barriers and reminds people that the speaker is, after all, human, too.

The secret to truly effective communication lies not in how much information you convey but in how deeply that information resonates with others. Humanizing your content means going beyond the surface and tapping into the shared language of humanity—the idioms, emotions, and experiences that are universal to all of us.

By incorporating idioms, sensory language, cultural touchstones, humor, and vulnerability into your writing, you'll be able to cut through the robotic noise and connect on a human level. These techniques will not only make your message more memorable but also inspire trust, emotional engagement, and loyalty from your audience.

The beauty of these humanization techniques is that they can be applied across any industry, any audience, and any message. Whether you're writing sales copy, telling your brand's story, or crafting an email, the power to humanize is within your hands.

By leveraging these often-overlooked secrets, you'll have the ability to create content that does more than just inform—it will inspire, connect, and make people feel something real.

The Humanizers Takeaway

When we're humanizing AI-generated content, we're not throwing the baby out with the bathwater. It's not about scrapping AI—it's about **enhancing** it. The AI gives you a starting point, but **you** provide the empathy, the emotion, and the storytelling that makes content truly connect. You are the one who takes that raw AI output and transforms it into something alive, real, and impactful.

So, here's your challenge: **Take your next AI-generated piece of content, follow these steps, and humanize it.** See the difference it makes in the connections you create—and the results you achieve.

Humanizing Doesn't Mean Starting from Scratch

Let's address the elephant in the room. You might be thinking, *"This sounds like a lot of work—why not just stick with the AI content?"*

Here's the reality: the process of humanizing content isn't about throwing away efficiency. In fact, it's the perfect blend of speed and authenticity.

Before AI, writers would spend **hours—sometimes days—crafting a single email** or sales letter from scratch. Brainstorming, drafting, revising, editing, ad nauseum. Every word had to be painstakingly considered. Now, you're starting with a base, a solid foundation that the AI has already provided.

You're not reinventing the wheel here—you're refining it. **Humanization doesn't mean more work; it means better work, faster.**

A Few Minutes of Humanization = Massive Results

When you consider the impact that humanized content has on your bottom line—better engagement, deeper emotional resonance, more meaningful connections—the extra 15 to 30 minutes you'll spend humanizing AI-generated content will feel like a small investment with massive returns.

In the grand scheme of things, this process is still a **fraction** of what it used to take to write compelling copy from the ground up. The AI has already done the heavy lifting—**it's up to you to breathe life into it**. And with every humanized piece of content, you're not just creating copy; you're creating trust, loyalty, and a lasting relationship with your audience.

Action Step:

Follow each step in this chapter and go through the process of humanization from start to finish. Observe how you felt and note the amount of time it took to complete compared to how long it normally takes you to use AI exclusively for a similar project. Note how there are intangibles at work here that offset any difference in time.

Chapter Twelve

THE ONGOING PROCESS OF HUMANIZED CONTENT CREATION

Content creation is no longer just about producing blog posts or social media updates. It's about crafting messages that **resonate deeply** with your audience. In the world of AI, content creation has become faster, but often, it's at the cost of **emotional connection** and **authenticity**.

This chapter will explore how you can consistently apply **humanization** to your content, even as you scale your content efforts so that every piece remains **meaningful** and **personal**.

Why Humanized Content Matters at Scale

When businesses grow and their content needs increase, many turn to AI to handle the volume. However, relying solely on AI can result in content that feels **detached** and **robotic**. As a Humanizer, your goal is to scale your content without losing the **personal touch**.

This is where humanized content creation comes in—it's about ensuring that no matter how much content you produce, each piece still feels like it's written by someone who **cares**.

When you humanize content at scale, you:

- Build **trust and loyalty** with your audience.
- Differentiate your brand from the overwhelming amount of generic, AI-generated content.
- Create a deeper **emotional impact** that turns readers into long-term customers.

Scaling doesn't have to mean sacrificing **quality**. With the right systems and strategies in place, you can maintain the human element in every piece of content you create.

How to Scale Humanized Content: Key Strategies

Scaling content creation while keeping it human requires a deliberate approach. Here are some key strategies to help you do just that:

1. Develop a Content Strategy Built on Empathy

Scaling humanized content starts with building a content strategy that's rooted in **empathy**. This means your content plan should revolve around the **emotional needs** of your audience, not just the keywords or topics you want to rank for. Ask yourself:

- What are my audience's biggest challenges right now?
- How can I speak to their emotions in a way that resonates?

Example:

Instead of starting with a list of keywords or content topics, start with a list of **emotions** your audience is likely to feel. Then, create content that speaks directly to those emotions.

For example:

- **Emotion**: Overwhelm.
- **Content**: "How to Simplify Your Workday Without Sacrificing Results."

When you build your content around empathy, every piece will feel relevant and human, no matter how many you produce.

2. Use AI as a Tool, Not the Creator

AI can be a valuable tool in your content creation process, but it shouldn't be the creator—it should be the **assistant**. Use AI for research, data analysis, and drafting content, but always make sure a **human** is refining and personalizing the final piece.

Example:

Let AI handle the initial draft of a blog post or social media update, but go in afterward and add the **human elements**—a conversational tone, empathy, and emotional storytelling. This way, you're still benefiting from AI's efficiency without sacrificing the **authentic connection**.

3. Maintain a Consistent Brand Voice

As you scale, it's easy for content to lose its consistency, especially if you're using multiple writers or AI tools. To keep your content feeling human and personal, you need to establish and maintain a **consistent brand voice** that reflects your brand's values and personality.

Example:

Develop a **brand voice guide** that outlines the tone, style, and emotional triggers you want your content to convey. This guide should include:

- The overall tone (friendly, authoritative, compassionate, etc.).
- Key phrases or messages that reflect your brand's values.
- Guidelines on how to address your audience's emotional needs.

Share this guide with your team and any AI tools you use so that all your content feels aligned and consistent, even as you scale.

4. Tell Stories, Even in Short-Form Content

Humanized content thrives on storytelling, but scaling often leads to shorter, more transactional content—think social media updates, email subject lines, or ads. Even in these brief formats, you can still **tell a story** that connects emotionally with your audience.

Actionable Example:

- Instead of writing an email subject line that says: *"50% off this week only!"*
- Write: *"Remember that dream project you've been putting off? Now's your chance to make it happen."*

This short-form content still tells a **mini-story** that taps into the reader's emotions and encourages action.

5. Engage in Real-Time Conversations

One of the best ways to humanize your content is by engaging directly with your audience through **real-time conversations**. Whether it's through social media interactions, live videos, or comments on blog posts, creating opportunities for direct communication adds a human touch that AI can't replicate.

Actionable Example:

- Respond to comments on your social media posts with personalized replies.
- Host live Q&A sessions where you can interact directly with your audience and answer their questions in real-time.

These conversations not only humanize your brand but also help you gather **real-time feedback** that can be used to improve your content strategy.

Scaling Humanization Across Different Content Types

As your content needs grow, you'll be producing various types of content—blogs, social media, emails, ads, and more. Here's how to scale humanization across different formats:

1. Blog Posts

For blog posts, scaling means publishing more content more frequently. But even as you increase volume, each post should still feel personal and connected to the reader's emotional experience.

Tip:

Focus on creating in-depth, valuable content that solves real problems for your audience. Use **case studies, personal stories,** and **examples** to add an emotional layer to every post.

2. Social Media

With social media, the challenge is producing enough content to keep your audience engaged without falling into the trap of posting generic, repetitive updates. Scaling humanization on social media means maintaining a **conversational tone** and interacting with your audience regularly.

Tip:

Use storytelling, questions, and interactive posts to foster engagement. Respond to comments and messages with personalized replies that show you're listening.

3. Emails

Scaling email campaigns can sometimes lead to cold, transactional messages. To maintain the human element, personalize your emails as much as possible and write them in a **conversational tone.**

Tip:

Start with a personal greeting, acknowledge the reader's specific pain points, and always offer value beyond the product or service you're promoting. Even in automated sequences, make the content feel **tailored** to the reader.

4. Ads

Ads tend to be short, which makes it harder to humanize them at scale. However, you can still make them feel personal by using **empathetic language** and focusing on the **emotional benefits** of your product or service.

Tip:

Use storytelling techniques to make your ads more engaging. Instead of focusing on the features, highlight how your product or service will improve your audience's life.

The Importance of Humanization as You Grow

As your content strategy scales, it's easy to fall into the trap of prioritizing **volume over quality**. But the true power of content comes from **connection**, and that's something that can't be compromised.

Even as you produce more content, your audience will continue to crave human interaction, empathy, and emotional resonance.

Scaling your content doesn't mean sacrificing the **soul** of your messaging. With the right approach, you can expand your content strategy while keeping it human, personal, and emotionally impactful.

Next Steps

Scaling humanized content is a balance between efficiency and empathy. As you continue to grow your content strategy, remember that it's not just about producing more—it's about maintaining the emotional connection that keeps your audience coming back.

In the next chapter, we'll dive into how you can humanize copy specifically for **social media marketing**, ensuring your brand's personality shines through every post, tweet, and update.

Action Step:

Look at your content creation process and identify one piece of content that could benefit from humanization. Whether it's a blog post, social media update, or video script, add more human stories, emotions, and personal insights. Track how this change impacts engagement and audience connection.

Chapter Thirteen

MASTERING HUMANIZED COPY FOR SOCIAL MEDIA

In a world drowning in noise, social media has become both the battlefield and the prize. Brands rise and fall here, fighting for attention in a content-saturated landscape. But most of them are missing the point.

They chase clicks, engagement metrics, and fleeting moments of viral attention. They forget the most critical factor—*human connection.*

And that's where you, the Humanizer, step in.

While the masses churn out AI-generated posts and recycled content, you understand that real impact rises above the noise and resonates at a deeper level. It's not about more content; it's about more *meaningful* content.

In this chapter we're dismantling the superficial approach, stripping away the formulaic methods, and rebuilding it with soul.

The Defiance of Humanized Social Media Copy

Let's get real for a second. Social media is engineered to keep people hooked—endless scrolling, mindless tapping, quick dopamine hits. But the real human connections that drive loyalty and trust? Those have been buried under a pile of metrics and clickbait.

Most marketers have sold out to the machine. That may seem harsh, but it's true. They think if they automate enough, blast out enough content, and tweak enough keywords, they'll "win" social media. But let me tell you something—they're actually losing.

Every automated post is just another drop in the ocean of sameness. What you, the Humanizer, bring to the table is <u>a refusal to settle for robotic engagement</u>. You know that the goal isn't just to be seen—it's **to be remembered**. It's to *connect.*

Humanized copy does three powerful things in this space:

1. **It stirs emotions**—making people feel something real in the digital void.
2. **It breaks the mold**—cutting through automation with a message that feels like it's spoken directly to one person.
3. **It builds connection**—because when someone feels understood, they don't just scroll past—they stop. They engage.

Crafting Refreshingly Human Social Media Copy

Humanizing your social media will help you reclaim the very purpose of social media—*connection.* Let's throw out the generic formulas and get tactical with how to stand out while staying human.

1. Start with a Provocative Hook

Forget clickbait—it's time to be bold. Your opening line should stop people in their tracks, not because it's flashy, but because it's real. Speak to the emotion that no one else is acknowledging.

Example:

- Instead of: "New product alert! 🚨 "
- Write: "Ever feel like the world is running at a pace you can't keep up with? Us too. Here's how we're changing that…"

This isn't about grabbing attention for attention's sake—it's about starting a conversation your audience actually *cares about*. You're not just another voice—they're waiting to hear from you.

2. Break the Fourth Wall

Most social media posts feel like they're shouting into the void. You, on the other hand, are having a one-on-one conversation. Your copy should feel intimate like you're speaking directly to one person. Make it personal. Make it human.

Example:

- Instead of: "Our new tool boosts efficiency!"
- Write: "Let's talk about what's keeping you up at night. You know that feeling when your to-do list keeps growing, and you're running on empty? We created this to help you fix that."

Don't write to an audience; write to *a person*. They'll feel the difference.

3. Tap Into Raw Emotion

The most shareable posts are the ones that strike a nerve. People don't share products—they share feelings. Get past the surface and tap into the emotion beneath.

Example:

- Instead of: "Our app simplifies your life."
- Write: "Imagine logging off at the end of the day with a clear mind, knowing you've taken back control of your time. How would that change your life?"

You're not just offering features—you're selling the *feeling* of using your product.

4. Tell Stories That Matter

The world doesn't need another generic post—it needs stories. Not just any stories but ones that reflect real people, real struggles, and real solutions.

Example:

- "Meet Jenna. She was overwhelmed, exhausted, and about to give up on her business. Then, she found our tool. Now, she's running things on her terms. What's your story?"

Stories resonate because they're human. They cut through the clutter and give people something to relate to. That's the kind of connection that outlives a scroll.

5. Ask Questions That Challenge the Status Quo

Forget the generic "like if you agree!" questions. Instead, ask questions that make people think. Challenge them. Get them involved in the conversation.

Example:

- Instead of: "What's your favorite productivity tool?"
- Write: "What's the one thing you'd change about your work-life balance if you could? Let's talk solutions."

When you ask deeper questions, you invite deeper engagement. That's how you turn followers into a community.

Platform-Specific Humanization

Let's break it down platform by platform:

- **Instagram**: It's all about imagery, but your captions are where you bring the soul. Use your visuals to grab attention, and then humanize the experience in the caption. Don't just talk about your product—talk about why it matters in *real life*.
- **Twitter**: Short doesn't have to mean shallow. With limited characters, use wit, empathy, or even defiance to stand out. Challenge people. Make them stop and *think*.
- **Facebook**: Lean into longer posts with stories, reflections, and open-ended questions. Let people get to know the real you, the real brand. Here, the personal touches make the difference.
- **LinkedIn**: Stay professional, but don't be stiff. Share industry insights, yes, but do it through the lens of personal experience. Your audience here is craving authenticity in a sea of corporate jargon.

Humanizing in a Metrics-Obsessed World

Likes, clicks, shares—they're important, but they don't tell the whole story. What matters is *connection*—and the only real way to measure that is by the depth of your engagement. Is your audience talking to you? Are they coming back? Are they remembering your brand, not just as a company but as something more human?

The goal is this: When someone sees your posts, they should know there's a person, not just a brand, behind them. Humanized content isn't just another marketing tactic—it's a revolt against the soulless automation of connection.

And in a world where everyone's fighting to be heard, humanization is your loudest voice.

Social media is a crowded space, but humanized copy is what will help you cut through the noise and connect with your audience. As we move forward, think about how you can bring more authenticity and emotion into every post, tweet, and update.

Action Step:

Choose one social media post to create or revise using the techniques in this chapter. Focus on starting with a relatable hook, using a conversational tone, and tapping into your audience's emotions. Measure the engagement you receive and note how the humanized copy resonates differently.

Chapter Fourteen

BRINGING IT ALL TOGETHER WITH THE SOUL FRAMEWORK

At the heart of humanized copywriting and content creation is the SOUL Framework, which, as we discussed earlier, stands for Sensitivity, Openness, Understanding, and Leadership. This framework guides every aspect of how you write, communicate, and connect with your audience, ensuring that the human touch is never lost— even in the digital world.

In this chapter, we'll explore how to apply the SOUL Framework to every piece of content you create so that your messages resonate deeply, build trust, and inspire action.

As we touched on earlier, the SOUL Framework is a roadmap for creating **empathetic, humanized content** that taps into the core of your audience's emotions and needs. Let's break down each element of SOUL and how you can use it to elevate your copy and content creation.

1. Sensitivity

Sensitivity means being aware of and responsive to the emotional needs of your audience. It's about **tuning in** to their current challenges, fears, hopes, and dreams—and writing from a place of deep understanding.

How to Apply Sensitivity:

- **Know Your Audience**: Start by deeply researching your audience. What are their pain points? What keeps them up at night? What motivates them? Sensitivity means understanding the **emotional undercurrents** of their experience.

- **Choose Your Words Carefully**: Sensitivity shows up in the language you use. Are your words gentle and supportive, or do they come across as pushy or insensitive? Always consider the emotional impact of your words.

Example:

Instead of: *"You need our product to stay competitive in today's market,"*

Write: *"We know how tough it is to stay ahead in today's market. We're here to support you every step of the way."*

By acknowledging the emotional strain your audience might feel, you're demonstrating sensitivity and empathy.

2. Openness

Openness is about being **transparent, honest, and authentic** in your communication. Audiences today crave authenticity—they want to know who you are, what you stand for, and why you do what you do.

Openness creates trust and shows that you're not just selling a product but that you genuinely care about their success.

How to Apply Openness:

- **Share Your Story**: Whether you're writing copy for your brand or clients, be open about your journey, challenges, and values. People connect with vulnerability and honesty.
- **Avoid Overhyped Claims**: Openness means being clear and truthful about what your product or service can achieve. Over-promising creates distrust, while transparent messaging builds long-term relationships.

Example:

Instead of: *"Our software guarantees results within 30 days,"*

Write: *"Our software is designed to help you streamline your business, and while results vary, many of our users start seeing improvements within the first few weeks."*

By being open about the process, you're managing expectations and building trust.

3. Understanding

Understanding means going beyond surface-level data to grasp the deeper motivations and emotions driving your audience truly. It's about meeting them where they are, not where you assume they are. Understanding requires active listening and a willingness to **step into their shoes**.

How to Apply Understanding:

- **Empathy Mapping**: Create an empathy map for your audience, detailing what they're thinking, feeling, seeing, and hearing. This will help you craft messages that address their core needs.
- **Anticipate Objections**: Understanding means knowing the doubts and fears your audience might have. Address these concerns proactively in your copy, showing that you understand their hesitations and have solutions.

Example:

Instead of: *"This service is perfect for everyone,"*

Write: *"If you've tried other solutions that haven't worked, we understand your hesitation. Here's why our approach is different and designed with your specific needs in mind."*

This level of understanding shows that you're not just offering a product—you're offering a solution tailored to their unique challenges.

4. Leadership

Leadership in copywriting and content creation is about being a **guide** for your audience. It's about taking them on a journey from where they are now to where they want to be—and showing them how your product, service, or message can help them get there. Great leaders don't push; they **lead with inspiration** and **clarity**.

How to Apply Leadership:

- **Create a Clear Path**: Your copy should lead your audience toward a solution, not overwhelm them with options. Be clear about the next steps, and make it easy for them to follow.

- **Inspire Action**: Use leadership to inspire confidence in your audience. Show them what's possible if they take the next step and guide them toward that transformation.

Example:

Instead of: *"Sign up now!"*

Write: *"Are you ready to take control of your business and see real results? Join us today, and we'll help you make it happen."*

This subtle shift in language positions you as a leader who is guiding your audience toward their goals rather than simply selling a product.

Putting the SOUL Framework Into Practice

Now that we've broken down the SOUL Framework, it's time to apply it to your copy and content creation. Here's a step-by-step approach to integrating SOUL into everything you write:

1. **Start with Empathy**: Before you write a single word, take time to reflect on your audience's current state. What are they feeling? What do they need from you right now?

2. **Be Transparent**: Approach your messaging with honesty and openness. Share stories, highlight your values, and avoid making exaggerated claims.

3. **Address Concerns**: Think about the doubts and objections your audience might have, and address them with understanding and compassion.

4. **=Lead with Confidence**: Show your audience a clear path forward. Use your messaging to guide them toward the transformation they're seeking, whether that's making a purchase, signing up for a service, or simply engaging with your brand.

The SOUL Framework in Action: A Real-World Example

Let's say you're writing an email to promote a new product. Here's how the SOUL Framework would guide your messaging:

- **Sensitivity**: Start by acknowledging the current challenges your audience is facing (e.g., feeling overwhelmed and looking for ways to streamline their work).

- **Openness**: Be honest about the product and its benefits. Share your journey in developing the product and why you believe it can help.

- **Understanding**: Address the common objections or doubts your audience might have about purchasing. Show empathy for their concerns.

- **Leadership**: End with a clear call to action that inspires confidence and shows them the path forward.

Next Steps

The SOUL Framework is more than just a tool for better copywriting—it's a guide for **building deeper connections** with your audience. As you continue to create content, always come back to these four principles: **Sensitivity, Openness, Understanding, and Leadership.**

When you infuse your work with SOUL, your audience will not only respond—they'll trust you, connect with you, and take action.

In the next chapter, we'll explore the future of humanized content and how you can stay ahead in a world where AI-generated content is becoming more prevalent. With the SOUL Framework as your foundation, you'll be equipped to navigate whatever comes next.

Action Step:

Apply the SOUL Framework to a piece of content. Walk through each step—**Sensitivity, Openness, Understanding, and Leadership**—and ensure that your content reflects each principle. Share the content and observe how it connects with your audience on a deeper level.

Chapter Fifteen

THE FUTURE OF HUMANIZED CONTENT IN AN AI-DRIVEN WORLD

As AI continues to advance, the landscape of content creation will undoubtedly evolve. AI tools will become more sophisticated, and businesses will increasingly rely on them to produce content at scale. But as AI-generated content becomes more prevalent, **humanization** will become more important than ever.

In this chapter, we'll explore the future of humanized content and how you can stay ahead in a world dominated by automation.

Why Humanized Content Will Always Have a Place

Despite the power of AI, there's one thing it can never fully replicate: the **human experience**. AI can generate text, analyze data, and simulate conversations, but it cannot replace the emotional depth and authentic connections that come from real human insight.

In the future, the businesses and content creators that succeed will be the ones that master the balance between AI efficiency and **human empathy**. Here's why humanized content will always have a place:

1. **Emotional Connection**: AI-generated content can be efficient, but it often lacks the emotional resonance that humanized content brings. People are driven by emotions, and they connect more deeply with brands and content that speak to their hearts.

2. **Trust and Authenticity**: As AI becomes more widespread, consumers will crave authenticity. They will seek out brands and content that feel real and trustworthy. Humanized content creates that **sense of trust** by being transparent, empathetic, and grounded in real experiences.

3. **Creativity and Innovation**: AI can generate content based on patterns and data, but true creativity comes from the **human mind**. The ability to think outside the box, tell stories in new ways, and connect seemingly unrelated ideas is something AI cannot do. Human creativity will continue to be a competitive advantage in the world of content creation.

How to Stay Ahead in the AI Era

To stay ahead in an AI-driven world, content creators need to leverage the strengths of both AI and humanization. Here are some strategies to ensure your content remains relevant and impactful:

1. Use AI as a Tool, Not a Replacement

AI is a powerful tool, but it should never replace the **human element** in content creation. Use AI to handle tasks like research, data analysis, and drafting content, but always add the human touch through **emotional insight, personal anecdotes,** and **empathy.**

Example:

Let AI generate a draft of a blog post but go in afterward to **personalize** it with human experiences, emotional stories, and conversational language that AI can't replicate.

2. Focus on Storytelling

Storytelling is one of the most powerful ways to create a human connection, and it's something that AI struggles to do effectively. As AI-generated content becomes more common, storytelling will be a key differentiator for humanized content.

Example:

Incorporate **personal stories, client testimonials,** and **real-life examples** into your content to make it feel more authentic and relatable.

3. Prioritize Quality Over Quantity

As AI makes it easier to produce content at scale, there will be an influx of low-quality, generic content. To stand out, focus on creating **high-quality, deeply humanized content** that offers real value to your audience. It's better to produce fewer, more impactful pieces of content than to flood the internet with AI-generated noise.

Example:

Focus on creating long-form, in-depth content that dives deep into a specific topic and offers **unique insights** that only a human perspective can provide.

4. Humanize Every Step of the Customer Journey

Humanization doesn't stop with content creation—it extends to every interaction you have with your audience. From social media engagement to customer support, every touchpoint should be infused with **empathy, understanding,** and **authenticity.**

Example:

Ensure your customer service interactions are personalized and empathetic. Respond to customer inquiries with **compassion** and **understanding** rather than relying solely on automated responses.

5. Stay True to Your Values

In a world of automation, your brand's **values** and **mission** will be what sets you apart. Stay true to your brand's identity and ensure that your content reflects those values. Consumers are more likely to engage with brands that share their values and demonstrate a commitment to authenticity.

Example:

Highlight your brand's core values in your content. Whether it's through blog posts, social media updates, or marketing campaigns, make sure your audience knows what you stand for.

The Evolution of the Humanizers Movement

As AI continues to evolve, so will the role of **Humanizers**—those who are committed to maintaining the human touch in content creation and business interactions. The Humanizers movement will play a critical role in ensuring that the **soul of communication** isn't lost to automation.

Humanizers will be the ones leading the charge, creating content that resonates on a deeper level, builds lasting connections, and drives meaningful action. Whether you're a content creator, marketer, entrepreneur, or business leader, your role as a Humanizer will be to keep the **fire of human empathy burning** in a world that AI increasingly drives.

Embracing the Future with SOUL

The future of content creation isn't about choosing between AI and humanization—it's about mastering the balance between the two. By using AI to enhance efficiency and humanization to deepen emotional connections, you'll be able to create content that resonates in ways that AI alone cannot.

As we move forward, the **SOUL Framework** will continue to be your guide. By infusing **Sensitivity, Openness, Understanding, and Leadership** into your content, you'll be able to stay ahead in the AI-driven world and build meaningful, lasting relationships with your audience.

The future is bright for those who can master the art of humanized content creation. As AI continues to advance, the role of Humanizers will become even more critical. By staying true to your values, focusing on empathy, and leveraging the SOUL Framework, you'll be equipped to navigate the evolving landscape of content creation with confidence and authenticity.

Safeguarding Creativity in the Age of AI

As we stand on the brink of a new era, AI is both a remarkable tool and, if left unchecked, a **potential thief of creativity**. It promises efficiency, scalability, and automation—things that, on the surface, seem like the perfect solution for modern business. But beneath that promise lies a quiet danger: the risk of **losing our creative essence**.

Like a thief in the night, AI has the potential to drain the soul from our work if we allow it to do everything for us. Creativity, once the driving force behind human progress, can become an afterthought in the pursuit of faster, easier solutions.

But here's the key: **AI doesn't have to steal our creativity**. It doesn't have to take away what makes us human.

The **hope** lies in how we use it. AI should be seen as a **tool**, not a replacement for the human spirit. By **harnessing its capabilities**, we can free ourselves from mundane tasks and give more time to the creative, empathetic work that only we can do. This is the balance we must strive for—allowing AI to assist us while **protecting the fire of our imagination**.

Humanization: The Path Forward

In this age of rapid technological advancement, it's easy to forget the most important aspect of communication: **the human element**. Algorithms may shape our feeds, and AI may automate our processes, but at the end of the day, **people connect with people**.

Humanization isn't just a buzzword or a strategy—it's a responsibility. Every word we write, every message we craft, and every interaction we have offers an opportunity to connect, empathize, and **breathe life** into the content we create. With AI-generated text often feeling mechanical and detached, it's up to us to infuse our work with the **authenticity and empathy** that only humans can provide.

Let this serve as a reminder: **Always humanize.** Whether you're writing a social media post, drafting an email, or developing a marketing campaign, think about the human being on the other side of that interaction. What do they need? How are they feeling? How can you make them feel seen and understood?

As AI continues to evolve, the challenge before us is clear: How do we keep the **fire of humanity** burning bright? The answer lies in each of us. Creativity, empathy, and connection—these are the flames that no machine can replicate. It's up to us to protect them, to nurture them, and to share them with the world.

The future may be digital, but the heart of it must remain **human.**

Action Step:
Identify one area of your business or content strategy where you can better balance AI and humanization. Take a concrete step to bring more human insight into that area, whether it's rewriting automated emails, adding personal stories to your marketing, or improving customer interactions.

Chapter Sixteen

RECLAIMING THE FABRIC OF LIFE

In all the rush toward efficiency and automation, there's something the world has forgotten. AI has dazzled us with its speed and precision, but in doing so, it has distracted us from something far more essential: the fire of our humanity.

This fire—our creativity, empathy, and the ability to connect—has been dimming, overshadowed by the lure of quick results and mass production. But here's the thing: the very fabric of life is woven from these intangible threads.

Chances are you didn't get into business because of transactions or optimizing performance metrics. Maybe you didn't want to change the world necessarily, but I'm guessing you wanted to make a difference in your part of it. And in doing so, to strengthen the invisible bond between humans—a bond that AI will never replicate.

We live in a world intoxicated by the pursuit of faster, easier solutions, where the subtle art of communication is often reduced to formulas, algorithms, and automation.

But the truth is, no machine, no matter how advanced, can weave the fabric of life.

No AI can feel.

No AI can create with passion.

And no AI can tell a story from the depths of a lived experience.

That belongs to us.

Here's the philosophical challenge we face: Are we willing to allow the relentless tide of automation to erode the very things that make us human? Or will we choose to stand defiant, protecting the fire of our creativity in a world that desperately needs it?

The reality is simple: AI is just a tool. An incredibly powerful one—but still a tool. The true power lies in the hands of those who dare to infuse their humanity into the work they create. Because when you strip away the convenience and the speed, what's left is this: an authentic connection.

And that's where the real magic happens. That's what stands the test of time.

Our creativity, empathy, and shared experiences are not commodities to be replaced by automation. They are the lifeblood of the connections we form, the foundation upon which true progress is built. Without them, the world becomes a colder, more mechanized place devoid of the rich textures that only humans can provide.

But this is not a lament; it's a rallying cry.

This is a call to action for all those who refuse to let the allure of automation overshadow human creativity and ingenuity.

It's not about resisting AI, as that would be futile. It's more about demanding that the tools we create serve to elevate us, not replace us. The future isn't a choice between technology and humanity—it's about ensuring that technology **enhances** the human experience, not diminishes it.

In this moment, we stand on the edge of something profound. We can either continue down the path of dehumanization **or rise up as *Humanizers*,** fiercely protecting the creative spark that keeps the world vibrant, alive, and meaningful.

The mission is clear: In a world increasingly driven by machines, we are the keepers of the flame. It's our responsibility to ensure that the fire of our creativity never goes out, to remind the world that the fabric of life—the human connection woven into every piece of meaningful content—matters now more than ever.

The future needs more than automation. It needs us.

JOIN THE HUMANIZERS

The Ethical Imperative of Humanizing AI: A Defiant Stand Against the Soulless Machine

Let's not mince words—AI has revolutionized the way we create, market, and communicate. It's efficient, scalable, and, at first glance, appears to be the perfect solution to every content problem we've ever had. But here's the uncomfortable truth: in our rush to embrace this shiny new tool, we're losing something far more important—our humanity.

We're at a crossroads. The easy path—the one most are already taking—is to let AI do it all. After all, why not? It's fast, it's convenient, and it's impressive. But convenience has a cost. And that cost, if we're not careful, is the soul of communication itself.

AI doesn't understand the human condition. It can't feel the pulse of a story, the nuance of a personal struggle, or the weight of a hard-fought victory. It can't empathize, it can't reflect, and it certainly can't care. What it *can* do is churn out content—an endless stream of words and data, polished but hollow, like a robot speaking in a human voice but never truly *hearing* the person it's talking to.

We have to ask ourselves: are we really willing to trade authenticity for automation? Is efficiency worth the price of human connection?

This isn't just about better marketing. It's about taking a stand. It's about rejecting the idea that more content, faster, is the answer to everything. It's about defying the cold, transactional nature of machine-driven communication and **demanding that we bring empathy, intuition, and creativity back into the process.**

Humanizing AI-generated content is more than a technique—it's an act of rebellion.

It's choosing to care when caring seems optional.

It's slowing down just enough to ask, "Is this how I would speak to a real person?"

It's refusing to let the machine replace the human heart.

But there's something even more insidious at play here. If we let AI handle everything, if we lose sight of our own muse—our creative spark—we risk sliding down a slippery slope. When creativity is taken for granted, when it's outsourced to a machine, it dims.

The act of creation, which should ignite passion and fuel our connection to others, starts to feel transactional. And slowly, almost imperceptibly, we lose touch with the source of our inspiration.

The muse doesn't shout when it's being neglected. It fades. It quiets down until one day, we wake up and realize we've forgotten how to tap into it at all.

This is the real danger. It's not just that AI will make our content sound robotic—it's that we, as creators, will become robotic ourselves. Once we've handed over the reins of creativity to a machine, getting them back won't be easy. Losing sight of our muse is a slippery slope that ends with us forgetting what made us creators in the first place.

If we let AI take over unchecked, we're not just outsourcing our content—we're outsourcing our ethics, our empathy, and our humanity. We risk becoming as robotic as the tools we use. And that is not a future worth accepting.

So yes, humanizing AI takes effort. It's not the quick fix that so many are chasing. But it's essential. It's a refusal to let the world become transactional and cold. It's a defiant stand for authenticity in a world increasingly obsessed with shortcuts.

Because the future of content creation isn't about how fast we can pump out words—it's about whether those words can still move us. **And if we lose that, we've lost everything.**

This is more than just a moment in time—it's the beginning of a movement. A movement of defiance, of reclaiming what it means to create, to connect, and to stand tall in a world that is losing touch with its humanity.

The Humanizers are not passive bystanders in the age of AI. We are the ones who refuse to let technology dull the edges of our creativity.

We are the ones who believe that, while AI may assist, **it will never replace the soul of who we are and what we do.**

We are the firekeepers, the storytellers, the ones who weave meaning into a world that too often feels cold and mechanical.

But this isn't a battle to fight alone.

We need each other. We need voices that will rise up and say, "Algorithms will not replace us." We need creators, thinkers, writers, and innovators who are ready to reclaim the power of their humanity in a landscape flooded with automation.

If you're ready to stand with us, to be part of a community that values depth over speed, empathy over efficiency, and connection over automation, then welcome to The Humanizers.

Humanizers: Assemble

This is your call to action. Your invitation to join a legion of people who are shaping the future—not by rejecting technology, but by demanding that it serves us, not the other way around.

We are the guardians of the creative spark, the protectors of the human connection that weaves through every word, every idea, and every story we share.

Together, we will rewrite the narrative of this AI-driven world.

Will you answer the call?

www.thehumanizers.com

As we move forward into this AI-powered future, the **Humanizers** will be the ones leading the way, **preserving the soul of communication**. This isn't a passive role. It's a movement, a **mission** to ensure that technology doesn't strip away what makes us human but rather enhances our ability to connect, empathize, and inspire.

You, the reader, are part of this movement. By embracing the principles of **Sensitivity, Openness, Understanding, and Leadership**, you are stepping into a role that goes beyond content creation. You are helping to shape the future—a future where AI and humanity coexist, not in competition, but in **collaboration**.

Become a Humanizer. Let your voice, your empathy, and your creativity shine through in everything you do. Inspire others to do the same.

Together, we can ensure that the digital world transcends efficiency and reclaims our **humanity**.

ABOUT THE AUTHOR

Andy O'Bryan is a seasoned direct response copywriter, AI content strategist, and thought leader in the emerging field of AI humanization. With over three decades of experience in the marketing and personal development industries, Andy has dedicated his career to helping entrepreneurs, coaches, and thought leaders create content that connects deeply and authentically with audiences.

As the co-founder of the AI Success Club, Andy embraced artificial intelligence as a tool for transformation rather than competition. He created the AI to Human Copywriting System to teach others how to humanize AI-generated content and bring empathy, creativity, and resonance to every message.

Andy's unique SOUL framework (Sensitivity, Openness, Understanding, and Leadership) has become a guiding principle for those looking to stand out in a crowded, automated marketplace.

In *The Humanizers: Breathing Life Into AI-Generated Content*, Andy shares his insights and practical frameworks for blending AI efficiency with the irreplaceable human touch.

This book is not only a guide to modern content creation but a call to action for anyone who values authenticity in an AI-driven world.

Andy currently resides in St. Augustine, Florida where he continues to innovate and inspire the next generation of content creators. When he's not working, you can find him walking on the beach.

www.ingramcontent.com/pod-product-compliance
Lightning Source LLC
LaVergne TN
LVHW051341050326
832903LV00031B/3669